STOP NOW!

REGISTER YOUR BOOK TO CLAIM YOUR $717.00 IN FREE BONUSES

I want to reward you for taking action and ordering this book. It shows me that you're serious and committed to growing your business, and I want to give you OVER $700 WORTH OF FREE BONUSES to help you really accelerate your growth.

Your FREE "Fast Action" Bonuses Include:

- Access to downloadable PDF version of this book, so you can print out and read anywhere! *[REAL VALUE: $29.00]*

- Access to over 2 hours of additional training in the 13 part video series where Mark walks you through the entire book, mind maps, and key takeaways. *[REAL VALUE: $297.00]*

- Access to downloadable PDF of the detailed mind map from the book - "*How to Maximize the ROI of Every Single Visitor to Your Online Store*" *[REAL VALUE: $97.00]*

- Access to the Previously-Unreleased video - "How to Access a VIRTUALLY UNLIMITED Database of your PERFECT Clients..." *[REAL VALUE: $97.00]*

- Free 30 Day Trial Membership & Access to our PRIVATE, "Members-Only" eCommerceSiteOwners.com "Platinum Elite" Coaching Program Website, where you can access the entire training program, including case studies, videos, tutorials, articles, marketing collateral, lead generation ideas, and MUCH more! *[REAL VALUE: $197.00]*

- ** Total REAL VALUE of Bonuses: *$717.00* **

To Claim your FREE Bonuses, it's simple! Just forward a copy of your order receipt email (*from Amazon or Barnes & Nobles*) to bookbonus@ecommercesiteowners.com. When we receive your receipt, we'll send you an email with the webpage to access your FREE gifts!

Copyright 2014-2015 – All Rights Reserved – eCommerceSiteOwners.com

All rights reserved. No part of this book may be used, reproduced, or transmitted in any form or by any means without the written permission of the author, except for the inclusion of brief quotations in a review.

The information contained in this publication is meant to serve as an overview of proven strategies that the author has employed to help business owners substantially increase their client base and revenue. The strategies and tips are only recommendations by the author, and reading this book does not guarantee similar results. Opinions are based on both personal experience and that of the author's clients.

Due to of the constant evolution of the Internet and unforeseen changes in the policies of social media/online/other companies, information contained in this book may become outdated or inapplicable at a later time. The author has made all reasonable efforts to provide current and accurate information, and the author will not be held liable for any loss or damage caused by unintentional errors or omissions.

Dedication

This book is dedicated to my beautiful, loving, and supportive wife, my three awesome boys, and my Mom and Dad.

Without their continued support, love, and patience, none of my successes in life would have been possible…

This book is also, of course, dedicated to my valued clients & students, whom I've been fortunate enough to work with over the last ten years.

Nothing makes me happier and gives me more personal satisfaction than helping you to grow your business to successes beyond your wildest imagination.

I appreciate each of you and look forward to working with you for many years to come,

May God Bless You and Your Family!

Mark Mattis

Table of Contents

Dedication	5
Table of Contents	7
Foreword	9
Introduction	13
CHAPTER 1: OVERVIEW	27
CHAPTER 2: UPSELLS AND CROSS SELLS	41
CHAPTER 3: AUTOMATED CART ABANDONMENT FOLLOW UPS	53
CHAPTER 4: EXIT POP-UPS	67
CHAPTER 5: ENTRY POP-UPS	77
CHAPTER 6: FACEBOOK AND TWITTER RE-TARGETING	97
CHAPTER 7: WEB RETARGETING	107
CHAPTER 8: BONUS "TRICKS" FROM THE PROS	119
CHAPTER 9: WHAT TO DO NEXT?	157
About the Author	161
What People Are Saying About Mark	163
Claim Your Bonuses!	181

Foreword

This book is for the hardworking entrepreneurs and small business owners who understand that in this day and age, the only real and sustainable way to build a successful business, is through <u>differentiation and providing the absolute best customer experience possible</u>.

Unless you're a massive big box store, with huge purchasing power, and unlimited amounts of advertising dollars to throw at marketing your product, it's no longer possible to compete on the basis of having the lowest price.

There is no future to be had in strictly selling "commodity" type products that are not discernably different from any of the dozens of competitors.

Business owners who choose not to adapt their retailing and marketing strategies, right now, to take advantage of the new & creative techniques that are now available to connect with your customers, will see that their businesses will compete at a significant disadvantage in the market.

With the powerful online tools and automated marketing systems that are now available to business owners, the world over, there's absolutely no reason why you cannot take control of your market, <u>by simply making your company, and</u>

the products you sell, the ONLY obvious choice. *Regardless of price.*

Success in the future of eCommerce and retail will hinge on you being able to implement a few simple strategies very well:

1.) Laser-targeting your marketing and advertising programs to focus 100% on attracting your ideal customer who embodies all of the characteristics, demographics, and *(most importantly)* buying behavior of your "best clients."

2.) Engaging with your customers *(and prospects)* in a more effective way - building deeper relationships through the use of a varied combination of personal interaction, online and offline marketing systems, and automated tools, software, and processes.

3.) Developing a clear and well-defined product marketing message, that succinctly defines a.) why your product is different *(i.e. better than all your "perceived" competitors')*; b.) why your customers & prospects should choose you/your company/your product over all others *(even at a premium price point)*; and c.) how your product will help them to receive their desired result, *faster / better / more easily.*

4.) Maximizing the value of each and every single prospect *(& customer)* that comes in contact with you, your company, your brand, your products, your brick and mortar retail stores, and/or your online store.

It is within this last point that we're going to be focusing on in the pages that follow.

As we begin, I look forward to guiding you through the complicated and often misunderstood world of eCommerce profit maximization.

My goal in this book is to help you to use the information presented to grow your business into whatever you want it to be.

Whether you own a physical retail store(s) and are looking to increase your profits by expanding online, or if you already have an online business, and are looking for a proven system to help you reach that next level of profitability and growth, this book will serve as your guide to the exact process that we use every single day in our *(and our clients')* businesses to dominate our markets.

Finally, I invite you to join me and your other eCommerce site owners inside the private community at eCommerceSiteOwners.com. You'll love it. I guarantee. **Now let's get started...**

Introduction

It was May of 2008, and I was still recovering from the sudden and unexpected death of my father, George Mathis, who had a massive heart attack, one year earlier, at our family's home in Hattiesburg, Mississippi.

I'd always been extremely close to my Dad, and we were best friends.

Over the previous few years, I'd been fortunate enough to come back into the family house plans business, to help out my father as he recovered from a stroke, while he was simultaneously battling diabetes and heart disease, the combination of which would eventually take his life.

At the same time, I was extremely excited to welcome my new identical twin sons – Ben and Grant – into the world.

My wife had a difficult pregnancy, and they were born a full six weeks early, which with twins especially, can be very problematic for their physical and mental development.

Due to their small size and difficulty breathing, they were assigned to the Neo-natal Intensive Care Unit (NICU) where they could be monitored more closely, 24 hours a day.

My wife and I were by their sides, constantly, as they struggled to gain the strength to move into a "normal" room, and out of the NICU.

However one day, we noticed they had severe fevers and weren't acting normally.

After some blood work and several other invasive tests, it was determined that they both had contracted meningitis, which if you're not aware of, is an extremely dangerous and deadly disease… *Especially in pre-mature infants.*

Over the next month, my wife and I traded time in the hospital, where we stayed by our boys' side, 24 hours a day.

She would stay during the daytime from around 7am – 5pm, and I would come at night *(after leaving my full time job)* and stay from 5pm till the next morning, when I would go back into work and try to be "productive".

By the way, at the same time, we also had our 3 year old boy at our house that we had to take care of / take to school / take care of HIS needs, while all this chaos was going on.

Thank God for my mother-in-law, being able to help us during those dark times. Her help was immeasurable.

As you can imagine, my (and my wife's) stress level was extremely high, we were worried about our twins and what effects the meningitis might have on their mental and physical development, and I was a zombie at work, due to my lack of sleep and excess stress.

If I'd worked for an outside employer, I would have been fired. No doubt.

I would have had no income and no time/energy to look for a new job, during this very expensive and stressful time.

That would have been VERY bad.

Fortunately, I had been blessed to have had my brother *(who I'm partners with in our family's house plan business)* working IN the business with me, where he was able to help me take care of many of the normal daily tasks that I would have ordinarily needed to get done.

If it weren't for his help during that period, its possible that our small family business, that supports many families, would have been forced to close forever.

Did I also mention that we had JUST bought a new house *(with a MUCH higher mortgage payment)* just over a month before before the babies were born *(6 weeks early might I add)?*

Oh, and that my family's business is in HOUSE PLANS, and we were just at the beginning of entering the horrific 2008 crash of the United States economy and construction industry?

Yeah, it sucked.

Hard-working families that wanted to build, couldn't get financing, and builders weren't building anymore spec houses, because they couldn't sell them.

Now, I'm certainly not sharing all of this so you can say "poor Markie", because I know, with complete certainty, that there are MANY people that were/are currently in much worse situations that I was in.

You, personally, might CURRENTLY be in a far worse situation that I was in…

If that's you, I want you to know that <u>I believe in you</u> and I hope that God's blessings rain down over you and your families' life… *I really do.*

The reason that I share all of these personal details with you, about my life during that period, is because <u>I want you to know where I was at</u>, when I started in eCommerce.

You see, I'm no different that anyone else. When I got started:

I had incredible outside stresses...

I was still recovering from the death of my Dad...

I was worried about whether or not my new twin boys were going to live or die....

I was worried about my older son...

I was worried about my wife...

I was worried about my mom...

I was worried about my family's business...

I was worried about the economy...

I was worried about money, and how I would pay for my new house and my family's expenses if my business went away, due to the economy...

I was beyond tired and exhausted, every single day...

I had absolutely NO time to do ANYTHING, especially try to learn about how to sell products online.

However, through all of this chaos, one important realization hit me like a ton of bricks.

<u>Something like this could happen again, and next time, I might not be able to save my business.</u>

Its at this moment that I made a conscious decision to **take true control over my family's financial future**, and invest in the education I needed to help me figure out how to develop a comprehensive strategy and plan to build sustainable and recurring income.

I needed to develop a new business that met several important requirements:

1. It should be location independent, where I can run from anywhere, with a laptop and high-speed Internet connection.

2. It should NOT require outside full-time salaried staff to run.

3. It should NOT require any sort of physical retail location or storefront.

4. It should be able to run on a flexible work schedule, without requiring me to be physically present from 8-5 M-F.

5. It should be operated online, and have the ability to use online tools, systems, and automated processes to minimize the amount of daily time needed to run the business.

6. It should not require any expensive equipment or large upfront inventory costs to get started.

7. It should sell a product or service that both I, and my family, could be proud of selling.

8. It should be something that could be automated and systematized in a way that would become a sellable asset, down the road.

This simple list of my criteria became my checklist that I used to evaluate online business opportunities.

After a few days of research, I knew that <u>selling physical products through an online store</u> was the route that I was going to try.

At that point, I had been selling some products *(mostly informational/digital type products)* for several years prior, but not really been super serious about it, and so they were making a few sales here and there.

I did A LOT of research and found this training course and community, called Stompernet, and these guys were the experts in selling stuff online, at the time.

One problem though… It was over $600 per MONTH to be a member, and as you can imagine at that particular time in my life, $600 per month might as well have been $6000 a month.

However, I believed in myself and I knew if I invested the money to get access to the right training, tools, mentors, and community, that there's no way I could fail.

I KNEW I was going to take action, and do whatever it takes to be successful. *With 100% certainty.*

Why? Because I had to. *There was no other choice for me.*

Long story short, I devoured the training. Implemented everything they told me to implement, and picked my first niche eCommerce market…

Ghillie suits. (Google it)

Now you might be asking, how did I come up with this market?

Well, I did some simple keyword research using free online search volume tools to verify that there was some demand there, but mainly I just thought it was a cool product that is hard-to-find LOCALLY for many people in the U.S. who don't live near a major metropolitan area.

Also, being from South Mississippi, where every single person you meet is a deer hunter, I knew that the product was something that had a group of people willing to buy this type of camouflage.

So I setup a website using the X-cart shopping cart, and found a drop ship supplier that could ship the products out for me when I made a sale.

I then undertook an EXTENSIVE search engine optimization (i.e. SEO) project to get traffic to the site.

I started making sales... A few here and there, but they were sales none the less.

Over the next few months, my little site would make the sales for me, 24/7, process their credit cards, and deposit the money in my checking account.

I would then email over the order information and shipping address of the customer to my drop ship supplier would pull the product, put it in a box, put on the shipping sticker, and send me the tracking number that I could then email over to the customer.

It was a super slick setup and I liked it...

The great thing about this new eCommerce site was that *I didn't have to go into debt to order a bunch of inventory* upfront, that I didn't know whether or not it would sell or not.

In addition, I didn't have to have an expensive storefront or retail location and pay for all the overhead, rent, utilities, and staff to manage.

I didn't even have to physically TOUCH the products. All I did was send an email over with the order information and the drop shipper's staff of employees did everything for me.

Basically, I just had to add my profit to the cost of the product from the drop shipper, and post the products on my site.

The difference in what the drop shipper charged me for the product (at a wholesale price) + shipping and what I actually SOLD it for, was my profit.

Then it happened…

You've heard the saying *"one is the loneliest number"*, and in the world of suppliers, that is absolutely true.

You never want to have only one source for a product line because that supplier then has you at their mercy.

Well, I had only one supplier, and I very quickly learned that they were NOT a good company to do business with.

Here's how I knew:

- They were CONSTANTLY out-of-stock on their most popular products. I would make sales and they couldn't fulfill, so I would have to refund the customers and lose their "good will". Hurting future sales, and wasting A LOT of my own time.

- They had HORRIBLE communication. No phone support *(phone would just ring and ring)*. 24 hour or longer turnaround on support emails. In addition, they were located two time zones away from me, and were never available in the mornings when we to get answers to our most important questions.

- They had absolutely NO CLUE on when they would get in new shipments of out-of-stock products, so it was impossible for me to save my orders by being able to give my customers a definite timeline for delivery.

- Worse of all, they became DIRECT COMPETITORS of me. Advertising the same products I was selling at much lower prices, with much better shipping timelines. It became harder and harder to compete since our pricing was significantly more, and I hadn't done a good job of differentiating.

As a result, after less than 8 months, I closed that business and basically just broke even on what it cost to setup and run. It was a failure, but I didn't give up.

From this failure, I had learned MANY important lessons, and gained immeasurable experience about selling physical products through an online store, so I started looking at new niche markets to enter.

From that point on, *the process got much smoother.*

I continued learning and investing in my education.

I built systems and used automated tools to start/run my sites and their marketing programs.

I found many great niche markets to start new stores in.

Most people would have quit, and many days I felt like quitting, as it would just be easier.

The reality of the situation was that <u>I was having many small victories</u>, every single day, and that was giving me the hope I needed to continue pushing forward.

A new sale on one of my websites…. a nice thank you email from one of my customers… a larger order from a person who had found my online store by just doing a search on Google. Being able to attend my son's school play, in the middle of a workday, without having to worry about asking my boss to get time off.

I just woke up each day and focused on working the plan that I'd developed the night before.

Small successes led to bigger successes, over time.

Constant, small improvements… made every single day… snowballed into huge positive improvements that helped me to <u>make more sales</u>, <u>improve my profits</u>, and <u>automate my businesses</u> in a way that I was very proud of.

I know this is probably the longest "Introduction" of a book you've ever read.

The reason I've shared all of this personal information with you, about my background and journey to get to where I am today, is because I want you to know that <u>I'm just like you.</u>

I followed a very long, very crooked road to get to here.

If a small town country farmboy from South Mississippi can do this, you can too.

I believe in you and am here to help you, every step-of-the-way.

Now lets get started!

----

* By the way, if you're wondering, my twins are completely fine today, and ended up having no permanent physical or mental issues as a result of the meningitis scare.

CHAPTER 1: OVERVIEW

"How to Maximize the Value of Every Single Visitor to Your Online Store(s), On Auto-Pilot"

When I was 7 years old in 1982, I was REALLY into a show called "The Fall Guy".

In the show, Colt Seavers *(played by Lee Majors, formerly the Bionic Man)* is a Hollywood stuntman turned bounty hunter.

Using his immaculate 1980 GMC 4X4 pickup truck, Seavers took down some of the most-wanted criminals on TV. From flying off jumps to ultra-dangerous high-speed pursuits, this truck did it all.

It featured a 6 inch-lift, 35-inch off-road tires, multiple off-road lights, a Warn winch and my favorite feature: the hidden compartment in the pickup truck bed to hide firearms and captured convicts.

Now, being a 7 year old boy that was really into the Fall Guy (and jacked up trucks), I had decided that when I got big, I wanted to be a stunt man too.

I mean, how hard could it be?

From what I could tell on the show you got to hangout with super hot blondes (like Heather Thomas - his sidekick on the show), drive around in your jacked up 4x4 (which, when growing up in South Mississippi was the equivalent of a Bentley), and do cool stunts where you never got hurt.

When I told my Dad of my plans, he said "Are you stupid? Don't you know that being a stuntman is extremely dangerous and can get you killed?".

Killed?

Up until that point, I had never actually thought about the "reality" of what being a stuntman really meant, because I didn't have a frame of reference or perspective.

I had no idea how many hours of training and experience actually went into learning that skill, and how they could potentially die (or at least be seriously hurt) by every single one of their stunts.

You see, what my Dad did *(in his own way),* was to share his knowledge and experience in the world to quickly let me know the reality of what a stuntman's life is really like.

He shared his "perspective" with me, let me know of some of the things I should consider (like possibly being killed every day you work), and helped me to save years of my time in training and probably tens of thousands of dollars in training.

The true benefit in having a coach and/or mentor, like my Dad was to me, is that they <u>save you incredible amounts of time and money by sharing their perspective and extensive experience in areas that you need guidance</u>... like in building and growing your eCommerce business.

Be sure to keep that important point in mind, as we get started...

Getting Started

Here's a quick overview of what you'll be learning in this book. The purpose of this training is to show you *how you can maximize the value of every single visitor to your website.*

Gone are the days when you can simply just send traffic to your site, and if they buy they buy; but if not, then you have no further interaction with them.

The "little known" and greatly-underutilized tips, tricks, and creative marketing techniques that you'll learn in this book can help you to dominate your competitors by building value and a much deeper relationship with everyone who comes to your site.

***INSIDER'S TIP:** As a business owner with a finite advertising budget, you have to be able to reuse and repurpose ALL of your traffic to maximize your profits, and ideally help to cover your new customer acquisition costs.*

Your visitors are your most valuable assets, because they CAN become your customers. It really doesn't matter whether or not they buy at the CURRENT time.

What you want to do is to build a deeper relationship with them, where they know, like, and trust you.

In the following chapter, you'll learn the *ideas* and *strategies* you need to accomplish your goals.

Make it Easy

You want to make it simple, quick, and frictionless to buy from you. The easier that you make it, the better,

You want to make sure that everything about your website very *easy to find, clear, and that your ordering process is "brain dead" simple.*

When they go through the checkout process, you're going to *present them with related value-added offers* that make sense for the type of product that they are purchasing.

Be There When They're Ready

You want to allow them to **buy when they are ready**. People often come to your website long before they're ready to buy. They don't know you, they don't know your company, and they don't know anything about your products.

That's just a fact of life, and when you realize that 98% + of the people that come to your site WON'T buy on that particular visit, then you can start to realize how important it is to capture these potential customer's contact information so you can continue to communicate with them, over a very long period of time.

As a result, you want to *capture their contact information* so you can *build a deeper relationship (and make lots of offers).*

Be Everywhere They Are

Don't be under the mistaken impressing that the only thing going on in your customer's life, is making the decision to buy your product.

They have a million different activities and issues going on in their lives, each and every day, and they'll be ready to buy your product… when they're ready to buy.

You can't FORCE someone to order, at the exact moment you want them to, however you can gently and constantly PERSUADE them to make that purchase decision a higher priority in their life, at that time, so that they'll take the desired action of completing the sale.

One of the true benefits of having a <u>proven and systematized marketing program</u> is that you're able to market to your customers in multiple ways, in multiple locations, and at different times.

For example, you may want to engage with them through Facebook, Twitter, Pinterest, LinkedIn, on different forums and websites, through email, through text messaging, through person-to-person phone calls, through automated phone calls, and/or through direct mail.

All of these different combinations of marketing outreach can positively affect your results dramatically, so you'll definitely want to test each, for your own online stores / your target demographics / product line, to see which one works the best for you and gives you the highest return on investment.

Commit for the Long Term

Marketing with consistency in communication, transparency, and professionalism builds trust with your customers.

As such, consistent followup is key.

Don't just let them come to your site one time and send them one email. You need to develop a systematized process for following up consistently, ideally on multiple different websites, *(for example, on Facebook, Twitter, via email marketing, via re-targeting, etc.)*

Your *messaging should be consistent, your contact information should be clear,* and *your offer should be persuasive,* and *centered around a definite deadline for action,* or else the special offer is gone.

Build Your Mailing List as a Valuable "Asset"

The most valuable asset of your business is your "mailing list" or your current customer list.

They are the people who are most likely to do business with you, both in the present, and in the future.

If you don't have contact information for a person who comes to your site, but leaves without purchasing, then you have absolutely no way to contact them in the future.

In the chapters that follow, you'll learn about the marketing techniques that we use to give ourselves the absolute best chance to capture that contact information from these type visitors.

INSIDER'S TIP: Think of these prospect lists as incredibly valuable assets, worth tens of thousands of $$$ that can be

utilized on future promotions and even new online stores, that you roll out.

When you have a new product that comes out, you can automatically email or promote that product to your existing list that already has a relationship with you.

Make this process of gathering your visitors email addresses and contact information a priority to your business and to your internal team.

Build YOUR Brand

One of the most beneficial techniques to maximize the value of the people on your mailing list, and to build deeper relationships, is through strategic brand-building.

For example, in your interactions, you should always be injecting some personality about who you are, what your company stands, and how they can use your products to make their life better.

The age of the nameless, faceless eCommerce store is over. Relationships formed with your clients can become one of the most valuable "informal" marketing systems that can radically increase your sales and profits.

From a strictly pragmatic standpoint, common sense would say that its *always easier to sell to someone who has a previous relationship with you* (and has hopefully had a positive experience), versus having to spend the time and effort to actively go out and acquire brand new cold traffic from sources like Facebook, Twitter, Google AdWords, or YouTube.

New leads that come into your system have to then go through the entire *relationship building process* to become comfortable with you and your company.

That process takes time, effort, and money that could be better utilized in focusing on selling more products to your EXISTING customer or "warm prospects" list.

Be a Real Person

As has been noted previously, people tend to do business with people they know, like, & trust.

In this age of huge faceless corporations that have absolutely NO tie to its customers, being seen as a "real person" can provide huge benefits to the small business owner.

I've personally seen this problem many times where the online store owners don't want to have anyone's name or face *(especially their own)* associated with a particular store, for various reasons.

I advise against going that route, as it prevents you from actively using one of your biggest advantages. That of "realness". That a customer can actually know from whom they are buying their products and services

Maybe you're a small family-owned business. Maybe you are Christians. Maybe you're really proud about YOUR product being made in the United States versus outsourced to a different country.

All these different elements can build into your story. *Integrate those touch points into your relationships and your follow-ups* with these different prospects to give them more reasons to deal with you, as an individual, versus a corporation.

There are already plenty of large corporate websites and "polished" online stores that you just know from the beginning that they're corporations.

They can tell that there's no *love* or *pride* that's put into the product.

Of course, that's a very generalized statement, however the main idea to understand is that most people want to do business with a person, a small family business, a business with a compelling story, etc vs. a large nameless, faceless corporation.

Take advantage of that reality.

Always Be Collecting Information

The more information you can get about a customer, the better, so if you can only get their email address, that's fine. However, you're going to have much better results if you're able to learn more about that customer and have the option of contacting them in different ways.

Ideally, you'd like to get their name, their email address, and their mobile phone number, which could then be utilized in both manual and automated text follow-up messages engage them more fully.

As you can imagine, text (i.e. SMS) messages have been shown to be highly effective, because people almost always open their text messages immediately.

In addition, with your prospects' mobile phone number, you can also implement "direct-to-voicemail" broadcasts and even "live" phone calls from your customer service team out to a customer.

One final point that can't be overstated is that <u>having the COMPLETE mailing address of your customers is incredibly valuable</u> because that gives you the opportunity to send out thank you cards, post cards, fliers, direct mail, and special offers that promote your products, thereby potentially increasing your profits even more.

In our company, we'll typically just start out by capturing our prospects' email address for a special "lead magnet" or unique and high-value offer or product that is developed, for the sole purpose, of generating enough interest (and intrigue) from your prospects so that they provide their contact information in exchange.

After you have that email address, you can then take them to a secondary page where you ask for all the more detailed information like mobile phone, full mailing address, full name, etc.

Having this information is hugely valuable and is an asset for your business.

ACT. NOW.

You want to *implement one or all of these techniques immediately*. Implementing even one new idea can make a dramatic difference in your business, however when you start to *layer these techniques* on top of one on another, it becomes a snowball that can really start to positively affect your profits.

Now, let's move on to the first way to maximize the ROI of all of your visitors to your websites, *upsells and cross sells*.

CLAIM YOUR FREE $717+ WORTH OF BONUSES RIGHT NOW by forwarding a copy of your order receipt email (*from Amazon or Barnes & Nobles*) to bookbonus@ecommercesiteowners.com.

When we receive your receipt, we'll send you an email with the webpage to access your FREE gifts!

CHAPTER 2: UPSELLS AND CROSS SELLS

"Want Some Fries With That?"

In my consulting and coaching programs, one of the major obstacles that we see cause issues for many "would be" eCommerce business owners is that they overanalyze EVERYTHING and they choose to wait until everything is 100% perfect, before moving forward and actually taking real action.

After having started and run dozens of businesses, and having worked in hundreds of different niche markets, I can tell you... without a doubt... that it will NEVER be perfect.

There will ALWAYS be issues with every market and every product. There just isn't a "perfect" market or product.

There will ALWAYS be competitors who have more money than you to market their products.

There will ALWAYS be issues that come up, every single week, that need to be addressed.

The most important characteristic of successful business owners that I've met *(and read about)* is that they make decisions based on imperfect information, and adjust as they go.

They consistently follow the path of "shoot first, aim later", where they choose to take massive action towards realizing their goals *(i.e. starting a new business)*, and then learn to fail fast so they can learn from the market, what it takes to be successful.

My favorite saying in business is "**Half-ass is better than no ass at all**".

What that means, *in my most eloquent South Mississippi language*, is that taking massive action is the best way to move forward and be successful.

Don't let not knowing all the details, up front, stop you from anything.

Do You Want Fries With That?

The quickest & easiest way to get started down the path of maximizing the value of every single visitor that comes to your website is through the use of strategic upsells and cross sells.

You've probably seen these on any most eCommerce sites that you frequent. For example, if you have every shopped on amazon.com or vistaprint.com, you will know immediately what upsells and cross sells are, as they are engrained profit maximizers used by the companies to increase their sales revenue, by recommending products that complement or enhance the product that you're currently buying.

To better define what these are...

Upsells *(from Wikipedia)* is "a sales technique whereby a seller induces the customer to purchase more expensive items, upgrades, or other add-ons in an attempt to make a more profitable sale.

Upselling usually involves marketing more profitable services or products but can be simply exposing the customer to other options that were perhaps not considered. *(A different technique is cross-selling in which a seller tries to sell something else.)* "

Cross sells *(from Wikipedia)* is "the action or practice of selling an additional product or service to an existing customer...

The objectives of cross-selling can be either to increase the income derived from the client or clients or to protect the relationship with the client or clients."

For example, one cross sell idea might be to offer ear buds, if your customer is already buying an iPhone case.

INSIDER'S TIP: Upsells and cross sells are one of the fastest and easiest ways to maximize total sales revenue on a per-order basis.

The beauty of this technique is that you're increasing the PPC, or "profit per customer", <u>with no additional cost of customer acquisition</u>.

As a business owner trying to drive traffic and new leads to your website, you will have already paid a given amount of money to get a customer or prospect to your website through pay-per-click advertising, an email list, video advertising, SEO, etc.

When that prospect is on your site, and they make the choice to actually purchase a product, even if it is very low margin product, you can present them with upsell and cross sell opportunities to <u>maximize the total revenue that you receive</u>.

This is a very important concept to understand.

Being that an order that was, in one moment, completely unprofitable, could go into being immensely profitable, by including nothing more than an automated system to make upsell and cross sell product offers to your existing traffic!

The beauty of this technique is that you don't have worry with the additional *(and unneeded)* cost of acquiring a brand new customer.

You are just selling more stuff to the same exact customer, at a much higher margin :)

Creative Ideas to Maximize Your Profits

There are a few time-tested ideas for you to immediately implement upsells and cross sells on your online stores.

The first idea is to just **offer 50% OFF a popular product as an initial offer**.

For example, if there's a product that costs you very little to produce, and you have a high profit margin, that's can be a perfect product for these type campaigns.

The next idea is to just **present complimentary products** - I mentioned that if they bought an iPhone case, you could present them with ear buds, a car charger, a wall charger, an extra cable, etc.

These upsell and cross sell products are other products that enhance the enjoyment of the product that they're already purchasing so they don't have to go around looking for all these items. You've taken the time to actually put them all together in a way that makes it very easy for them to just throw the extra items into their cart and purchase everything all in one place.

You can also offer "better" versions of products. Maybe you have a *silver, gold,* and *platinum* version of a particular product. For example, it might be a larger size or a different color, or it might have different (i.e. "improved" features) than their original product.

Your customers <u>might not know that the "better" version of their product exists</u>, but they'd be willing to upgrade their order to this higher margin, higher dollar-value version of the product that they are already buying, <u>if you show it to them</u>.

How To Implement In Your Own Store

There are several different ways that you can implement upsells and cross sells in your online store.

One of the most popular methods is to simply **add the pop-up when your customers are adding a product to the cart**.

For example, when they are on the product detail page, they would click "add to cart" button, and there would be an intermediate pop-up that shows up and gives them an offer for the upsell or cross sell product, BEFORE taking them into the shopping cart with the previously selected product.

A second way to implement would be to include **pop-up in the shopping cart itself**.

For example, after they've added all of their products to their cart, and they click the "check out" button, they are THEN presented with the upsell or cross sell, right before going into the order confirmation screen.

As a third method of implementation, you could even just **display the upsell or cross sell products on the actual product detail page.** Typically in the "product options" area or below the product information.

This type of functionality is generally included as a standard feature in most of the more popular shopping cart solutions.

In addition, within certain shopping carts, you can offer **one-click upsells IMMEDIATELY AFTER the initial order has been completed.**

For example, after your customers have completed the order process, and they've checked out, they are taken to a page that confirms your receipt of their order information, and gives them the opportunity to add a particular item or service on top of the existing items that they've just purchased.

The true power of this technique is that, in most cases, they won't have to re-enter their credit card information as its already been saved, and you're just basically "adding additional items" to their previous cart.

Several higher-end shopping carts like Infusionsoft offer this functionality, out-of-the-box, while other shopping carts will need to be custom programmed to handle this functionality.

The beauty of this upsell method is that you're not disturbing the sales process, and you make the process super simple and quick for the customer.

All they have to do is just make a very small decision to add a product or service to their order, and the new product can be shipped out with that previous order that they've just placed.

Auto-Pilot Upsells Via Email

One of the next marketing techniques that you can implement, in conjunction with your upsell and cross sell program is that of a well-written and timely **follow up email sequence**.

For example, you may develop a "new customer" sequence based around certain product categories or certain specific products, where you can say something like, *"Hey I see that you've bought this other product. People like you, who bought this product, also liked these products."*

Within that email sequence, you can then have links directly back to the product's page on your online store.

INSIDER'S TIP: You can even "pre-populate" the cart with a BUNDLE of products that are complimentary to that particular product they've just purchased.

With this type setup, you can generate new sales, on autopilot through your email system, simply based off what they have currently purchased.

Now, if they went through the entire checkout process on their original order, but did not take any other upsells or cross sells, *(or maybe not all of them),* you still have an opportunity to close those additional sales, after the fact, through your email follow-up sequence.

In our online stores, we typically do these follow up sequences from <u>seven to twenty-one days after their original purchase</u> to give ourselves the best opportunity to make those next few sales.

In addition, we've found that making **outbound phone calls** to our customers can be extremely effective for maximizing the total dollar value of each order.

For example, we'll actually call the people up after they place the order, and if we see that they didn't take advantage of all of our upsells or cross sells - or at least not our most popular ones, we will call and say something like:

"Hey, we just wanted to let you know that we got your order. Everything looks great from our side, we just want to let you know about one item that most people who order this product end up getting, and that is the XYZ product.

"If you'd like us to include that in your package, all we need to do is just get the go ahead from you. We'll just automatically charge your card for that and include it in the package that we ship out later this afternoon."

That's a very compelling message because the upsell process is so *simple and logical* to the customer. You're making it as easy as possible.

Lets review...

Your customers know, first of all, that you've received their order.

They know that everything is okay with their order.

And best of all, they know that the company is "real" - there's a real person behind the website actually answering the phone.

These three confirmations provide your customers with a sense of comfort and security. And best of all, you've made it very easy for them to purchase more stuff.

You should definitely consider that outbound phone call, especially if you are running just a few dozen sales a day. It can make a tremendous difference in the profitability of your store, and again, it helps demonstrate your commitment to the highest levels of customer service.

How to Get Started

Many times the functionality to do upsells and cross sells is already built into the shopping cart, or it can be custom programmed.

However, for most major shopping carts platforms, there are many low-cost upsell/cross sell apps that you can buy on a one-time basis or on a monthly type basis, that provide all this type of advanced functionality.

In my opinion, they are definitely worth the cost. It's one of the best values out there for maximizing revenue in your online store.

Finally, be sure to study amazon.com and vistaprint.com. They are two of the best at upselling and cross selling. Look at the language that they use, and look at the layout of their pages. Look what happens to you through email after you buy, or when you even visit one of their pages.

For example, on Amazon, they cookie your browser so they can send you re-targeted advertisements on all the other websites that you go to, many times on the exact product that you are looking at. They also do a lot of upselling and cross selling on the emails that they send you on a weekly basis as well.

And at Vistaprint, if you've ever gone through the process, can take 10 minutes to get through all the upsells, so you really have to pay attention to what you're doing to make sure that you only purchase what you're looking to purchase. They are two of the best; definitely check them out.

Now, let's move on to the second way to maximize the ROI of all of your visitors to your websites, *automated abandoned cart followups*.

GET INSTANT ACCESS TO OVER 2 HOURS OF PREMIUM VIDEO TRAINING THAT ACCOMPANIES THIS BOOK!

Just forward a copy of your order receipt email (*from Amazon or Barnes & Nobles*) to bookbonus@ecommercesiteowners.com.

When we receive your receipt, we'll send you an email with the webpage to access your FREE gifts!

CHAPTER 3: AUTOMATED CART ABANDONMENT FOLLOW UPS

"Did You Forget To Complete Your Order? Oh, let me help... :)"

Several years ago, when I was just starting up my marketing agency – Local Marketing Labs – I happened to be contacted by a local dentist, who had found my company on Google.

He said that every search he would do, regardless of the "local marketing" type search terms he would use, would return my company / our website as the #1 - #6 results, and so he figured I must be the best company to work with in the local area.

Which, of course, we were... :)

In any case, we talked on the phone and I arranged to drop by his office the next afternoon, so we could talk about what he was looking for, and how we could potentially help him with our services.

Now, keep in mind, that this is right at the beginning of my opening this new agency, and he was the first dentist I had actually met about potentially helping them with their marketing.

As a result, I had some preconceived (albeit unfounded) notions that his office would be nice, clean, and modern space with a friendly staff of knowledgeable professionals.

That was, unfortunately, not the case...

When I pulled up, there was exactly one car in the front parking lot, which is NOT what you would expect to see from a leading orthodontist.

The building was a 1971 brown color, and looked dirty, unmaintained, and generally unappealing altogether.

Despite my better judgment, I went into the office waiting area and was IMMEDIATELY greeted by the smell of dog or cat poop. Not sure which, but it was so bad, I almost gagged. Seriously.

In addition, the floors and furniture of the waiting area, looked *(and smelled)* as though those same dogs and cats and used them as a litter box.

I should have turned around, but again, <u>I obviously lacked good judgment on that day.</u>

I went up to the receptionist, and the lady was opened the glass window and asked how she could help me, and I said I had an appointment to talk with Dr. X about his marketing program.

She said he's currently with a patient, but she would go tell her that I was here.

Thirty minutes later, the rude dentist then had her summon me to the back area. Thinking we were going into his office or into a conference room, you can imagine how surprised I was when he wanted me to come by his dental chair WHILE HE WAS WORKING INSIDE ONE OF HIS PATIENT'S MOUTH!

I said, are you sure this is an OK time? I can certainly reschedule for a time that's better for you *(i.e. Never. I wanted to get the hell out of there, as quickly as possible)*.

He was like, *"Oh, no, this is a perfect time."*

So, I try to start asking him about his business, what types of marketing was he doing currently, what was working, what wasn't, what was his ideal patient, etc., all the while, he is DRILLING the poor patients teeth.

Picture this... The dentist is a very large man, and is leaning over the face of this young lady who is apparently having some sort of painful (and loud) procedure done.

She winces in pain, with every move he makes, while he continues talking to me like this situation is totally normal, and not at all strange.

Every time I try to talk or answer one of his questions, he starts up the drill and starts working on her teeth, while he's "listening" to me...

"Yes, Dr. X, one of the ways we can get more exposure for your practice is to...." WHIIRRRR, WHIRRRRR, WHIRRRR!

Loud drilling, woman grimacing in pain, dentist not listing to a word I'm saying, while the office smells like a construction jobsite port-o-let.

It was horrible.

Finally, the dentist finished up with his patient, and we went in his office to continue our "talk".

Within five minutes, he explained that his business was in the toilet, he was being sued by his old partner, and that he was in tax trouble and owed the IRS several hundred thousand dollars.

Yes, I know what you're thinking.... He was an "ideal" client for me...

Not so much.

God's mercy finally allowed the meeting to end, and I got out of there as fast as I could, vowing NEVER to interact with that person again.

The moral of the story is that, you can't force someone to buy anything AND everyone isn't your ideal customer. <u>You have to learn to more closely target your ideal customer, and then just to be there, in front of their face, when they're ready to buy, on their own timeline, whenever that might be.</u>

How to Be There, When They're Ready to Buy

In our and our clients businesses, the automated cart abandonment follow up system is one of my absolute favorites, because it allows you to provide a simple, quick, and easy way to *"be there when you're customer is ready to buy",* by sending them automated and prewritten follow-up emails/text messages/and even phone calls with a link back to their exact shopping cart that they left without purchasing.

Think about this...

Someone has actually been to your website; but not only visited, they've actually added something into your cart, and just not completed the order for whatever reason.

Well-timed and clearly-written followups with these customers can be tremendously powerful (and profitable).

First of all, customers have raised their hand. They have basically said, *"Hey, I like this product, I like you, I like everything about you. But for some reason I haven't been 100% sold enough to actually purchase the product."*

So, they're saying to you, *"I want to be sold, give me a reason to actually buy from you."*

Next, other than people who have actually purchased from you, these are your number one best prospects.

INSIDER'S TIP: There's no better money that you could possibly spend in your business, than by following up with these types of people. There are out-of-the-box apps and online tools that will do this process for you, automatically, based on certain time schedules after they add items into the cart.

Why People Abandon You

The next important distinction is for us to talk about exactly why cart abandonment happens.

First of all, **life happens**. Now, if you have any family or kids or a spouse, you know many times that you can have something that you're looking to buy. You have it in your cart. Maybe you're at home, and it's nighttime and for whatever reason, your kid comes in and they're scared of the "boogie man", or your wife needs you to come look at something, or whatever it might be.

The bottom line is that they got distracted during the checkout process.

"Life happens", and unfortunately, your product is not the most important thing in their lives.

You need to look at it from their perspective, however you do NOT want to just "leave it to chance" for them to *find your website again, find that product, add it to the cart, add in their credit card information, and then purchase at some point in the future.*

INSIDER'S TIP: You need to be Proactive and take the steps necessary to bring them back into your store to complete their purchase.

You want to take control of that process and remind them exactly where they were, what product they had, and give them a reason to buy now.

Many times you'll find that cart abandonment doesn't always happen because your prospects *don't like you* or they *don't trust you*, or they *don't like the product*, or *because they got buyer's remorse before they even purchased it.*

It's just that life happens.

Why You Gotta Make It So Hard

Another big reason why customers abandon checkouts is due to a **difficult or confusing checkout process**.

I've been through websites, just in the last week, where it's incredibly difficult and confusing to go through the checkout process.

For example, they require accounts to be set up originally, or they include very high shipping prices.

A few other reasons why people bail out of shopping carts is due to the fact that, perhaps it's not clear to your customers what happens when.

These type issues can typically be typically be solved by the business owner by just following eCommerce "best practices".

For example, if you're using a premium shopping cart solution like Shopify or Big Commerce, they have really great website templates available that are already designed with best practices in mind.

INSIDER'S TIP: Don't go reinventing the wheel, just use what works.

Make it Clear & Easy-to-Find

The next major issue that can cause your customers to abandon their shopping carts is that the **shipping information wasn't clear, or shipping simply cost too much.**

In general, people have become accustomed to getting free shipping online.

Now, offering free shipping may or may not be possible for you. However, at the minimum, you need to make sure that your shipping information is clear and easy-to-find.

For example, simply including verbiage on your store that says exactly how fast will they receive their order with their different shipping options, and exactly what is the cost of each one, is a great place to start.

Generally speaking, just make sure that your shipping information is very visible, it's clear, it's descriptive, and that it makes it very easy to figure out exactly what's going to happen.

Next, your **return and exchange information might not be clear and/or easy-to-find on your store**.

Your customers and prospects want to know if they have a problem or they don't like that particular product or it doesn't work for them that they're going to be able to get their money back.

INSIDER'S TIP: Don't try to hide this information, just make it a pop-up link that opens up in a new tab so you don't take them away from their checkout page.

Another area that can cause major issues for cart abandonment is when the **customer service phone number and contact information is hidden**.

Now, this is huge. Your customers want to know that they have direct access to a phone number and a real person behind that phone number that they can call if they have any questions.

From our personal experience in all of our online stores, we've found that our customers usually won't even call the phone number, to get a question answered initially. *They just want to know it's there.*

Successful online store owners make it a priority to have a "contact us" form, an email, a fax, and ideally a 1-800 phone number for their customer service team.

In addition, if you can show headshot pictures of the people who are answering the phone, or members of your team, that's great as well.

Am I The First Person to Ever Buy This Product?

The next major issue that can cause customers to abandon their shopping carts is that there is **no social proof** that others have ordered the product, used it, and been happy with the results.

For example, if you are able to highlight previous customers who have actually used your product and left a testimonial/review, that will make your new prospects feel much more comfortable that they're not the very first one to ever buy this product.

INSIDER'S TIP: In our own stores, we try to put testimonials on the top each of those checkout pages, just to let our customers know that there are real people that have actually bought this product and were happy with it. They're telling in their own words exactly what their experiences have been with our company. And best of all, YOU can choose whichever testimonials you want to use.

EMAIL FOLLOWUP SYSTEMS

As you rollout your abandoned cart follow-up system within your shopping cart, you may also want to implement an **automated EMAIL follow up system**.

Again, many shopping carts have automated abandon cart follow up systems in place that you can turn on, for free or a small monthly fee.

In our own online stores, we will typically just choose a lower tier of the shopping cart package, a cheaper monthly plan, and then we have different apps that we use that are very low one-time cost, or very low cost monthly, that do a little bit better job and allow us to have a little more flexibility on how we time the messages, what we say, and how we customize our messages.

For example, we're able to basically customize the messages that go out and the schedule at which they are triggered.

INSIDER'S TIP: When your customer actually orders for that very first time, that's when the work begins. Our goal then is to build that relationship with them to get them to be a long-term customer, and get them to come back more often and buy more. Get them to refer us to other people, and to again build that relationship.

In your follow-up email sequence, you'll want to include a link in all emails to send the customer directly back to that pre-populated cart <u>with a deadline</u>.

Even if the system does not really remove those items from the cart after a certain deadline, you'll <u>definitely want to include an explicit deadline to complete the purchase</u>, or it becomes an invalid offer.

Maybe it's 24 hours, which we typically use, but I wouldn't recommend any longer than 72 hours after the items were initially put into the cart, as we've found that timeline to be the "sweet spot" where we see the best successes.

To reiterate on one important point from above, be sure to **include a deadline in every one of your emails**, with explicit verbiage, to make sure that they know that that the price or the item will be going away or not available after that point.

INSIDER'S TIP: Five or six years ago, we had to custom program all of this stuff into our shopping carts. It was extremely complicated, very time consuming, and very costly. We were able to get exactly the functionality that we were looking for. However, when the shopping cart updated their software, we would have to constantly go in and update that custom code, so it really was a pain. I definitely don't recommend anyone doing that.

The solutions that are out there now are so good, that there's really no reason to custom program, unless you're just using a specific cart that does not have apps or that functionality available to them. With all the shopping carts that we recommend, mainly Shopify and Big Commerce, there are low cost apps out there to manage this process.

I'm not noting specific apps, because we change which ones we like all the time, because there's new ones coming out all the time that do a little bit better job for less money. You can very easily research that for whatever shopping cart you use, however if you'd like to know my specific recommendations right now, just send me an email :)

Now, let's move on to the third way to maximize the ROI of all of your visitors to your websites, *exit pop ups*.

DOWNLOAD YOUR FREE PDF VERSION OF THE MAXIMUM PROFITS BOOK + ALL OF THE DETAILED MINDMAPS!

Just forward a copy of your order receipt email (*from Amazon or Barnes & Nobles*) to bookbonus@ecommercesiteowners.com.

When we receive your receipt, we'll send you an email with the webpage to access your FREE gifts!

CHAPTER 4: EXIT POP-UPS

"Don't Leave Before I Give You Something Special..."

On January 1st, 1962, The Beatles were involved in a, now-famous, audition for Decca Records at their Decca Studios in West Hampstead, north London, UK.

This was before The Beatles had reached international stardom, and their manager Brian Epstein had already made numerous trips to London to visit record companies with the hope of securing a record contract, however they were continually rejected by many of the top record companies including Columbia, Pye, Philips, and Oriole.

On that day, Paul McCartney, John Lennon, George Harrison, and Pete Best were auditioned by Decca staff and performed a total of fifteen songs in just under one hour. Epstein and the Beatles decided on a selection of covers the Beatles had performed in various clubs over the years, along with three Lennon–McCartney originals.

After completing the session, the Decca sound engineers and talent scout told them them he "could not see any problems and he would let the group know of his decisions in a few weeks."

Eventually, Decca Records rejected the Beatles, saying "guitar groups are on the way out" and "The Beatles have no future in show business."

Decca instead chose Brian Poole and the Tremeloes, who auditioned the same day as the Beatles, as they were local and would require *lower travel expenses*.

[parts excerpted from Wikipedia.com]

This session is considered one of the biggest mistakes in music history, as The Beatles, of course, went on to become one of the most popular bands in the world.

The moral of the story is that, you never know who a stranger you meet is going to turn out to be.

Give them the benefit of the doubt, and ALWAYS put your best foot forward.

As a small business owner, this means that you need to "cast a wide net" and capture the contact information of ALL prospects who come to your online store, so you can build relationships & make offers.

You never know which of your visitors could turn out to be "bigger than The Beatles" and place a very large order and/or connect you with a major account.

How To Use Exit Popups To Maximize Your Income

The next marketing technique that we use, both in-house and on the stores of our clients, to maximize the return on investment of every single visitor that comes to your website is through the use of Exit pop-ups.

Now, if you're not familiar with this technology, they are basically unblockable pop-ups that occur when the software determines that a person is attempting to leaving a site.

Basically, the underlying technology tracks the behavior of your visitors' mouse and cursor on their screen, so that it can be determined when they are about to close out that browser window or go back into their browser's URL window to go to a different website.

When the software senses this type of activity, it can track that, and it will automatically trigger an exit pop-up window (*that's unblockable*) to present your visitors with an offer.

Now, you might be saying "Mark, I hate those type windows and I don't want to put those on my website because it irritates my customers."

Then Mark will say "I agree. I don't like popups either, but the proven fact is that they work. As a result, I'm going to use them on every single one of my sites until they stop working. If you don't choose to use them, just be OK with not making as many sales as you could, because you won't."

Give Us a Chance to Prove Ourselves

When you're implementing innovative new technologies like Exit Popups, the entire purpose is just to get that first interaction with a customer.

Your primary goals with capturing their contact information in this way is it allows you to introduce them to you, to your products, and to have the ability to tell them why your company and you are different from all the nameless, faceless corporations out there.

INSIDER'S TIP: *Hopefully, throughout this process, you can build a relationship with them that's long term, where they buy a lot of stuff over time. They refer their friends and family, and you get to show them the high quality of your customer service.*

When getting started, one of the first ways that we recommend using the exit pop-up is for promoting a **time-sensitive special offer**.

Within our businesses, we try to implement this on each and every one of our online stores, and we rotate this offer so that our customers do not tire of the same messaging.

Your offer might just be a *certain dollar amount off your order*, or a *percentage off of your total purchase*.

It might be *free shipping, where they get a special code from us*.

It might be a *special bonus - buy one, get one free*.

You can even use the pop-up to have them *join your newsletter or your coupon club*, or to download a special report or another product that would be beneficial to your target demographic.

The specific option that you choose will depend on the particular market and the type of products that you're offering, but it needs to be very *simple, straightforward*, and *to the point*.

For example, your offer could be something like "Opt in to get this information," and then you send them to a simple page where they can get it.

On that page, you then put a time sensitive offer - "This is only valid for the next 24 (or 48) hours," or whatever it might be.

By including a deadline, you're giving your prospects a valid reason to buy now (or take action / download / etc.).

Ideally, through this process, we want to collect the email, and/or mobile phone number and/or mailing address, for our prospect.

That might not always be possible, however if they take the next step to actually add their phone or their full name, or even their mailing address, then they're qualifying themselves as potential customers that are serious.

Treat them differently than the "freebie-seekers".

INSIDER'S TIP: One technique that we do is to ONLY ask for the email on the very first pop-up, to make it simple and less overwhelming. After they add their information, we THEN send them to an intermediate page, where we then ask them for the additional information, like their mobile phone number or their mailing address, or their full name. Getting this additional contact information really gives you alot of opportunities to do some really creative follow up, in multiple ways.

IDEAS FOR YOUR FOLLOWUPS

One marketing technique that we use extensively with our exit popup promotions is to include text messaging, where we can automatically send special offers and messages, directly to their phone.

In addition, once we have their mobile phone number, and they've confirmed that they do want to receive messages from us *(for CAN SPAM compliance)*, we can also send voice broadcasts, alerting them to new offers and products that we're promoting.

Of course, when we have their mailing address, we can also do physical mailing pieces, direct mail flyers, etc.

INSIDER'S TIP: A great way to use direct mail and postcards might be to have special sales around holidays like Thanksgiving or Christmas or Black Friday, or maybe our valued customer sales, or sales on different product categories or products.

In everything that you do, be sure to include opportunities to connect & build a relationship with your prospects through education.

Also be sure to provide additional ways for them to stay in touch through your Facebook page, Twitter, YouTube, your podcast, etc. The point is that you want to allow them to interact with you and learn more about you and your <u>business in whatever way they feel comfortable and on whatever timeline that works for them.</u>

The entire purpose of the exit pop technique is that you don't want them to come to your website and leave empty handed.

You want to give them something of value, and get their permission to start building a relationship with them.

DON'T FOLLOWUP JUST ONCE

In our testing, we've always found that it's generally best practice to follow up multiple times, ideally through different marketing channels like email, SMS, phone, or direct mail. In addition, we generally try to setup a 10 day follow-up sequence, where the content and offers will vary depending on the store we're promoting and its target demographic.

INSIDER'S TIP: *The follow up that we do is just based on building a relationship. It's not sales-y at all, but we will make two or three offers during that ten day period, and we will remind them about any deadlines for taking action. The main point is just to introduce them to us and our business. If they buy nothing during that ten day period, then they're at least on our house list for future promotions.*

In closing exit pop-ups are very effective tools to allow you to take advantage of traffic that originally comes to the site, and for whatever reason, are looking to leave the site without opting in or purchasing. We want to capture their information and give them a reason to do business with us.

I'm not noting specific apps, because we change which ones we like all the time, because there's new ones coming out all the time that do a little bit better job for less money. You can very easily research that for whatever shopping cart you use, however if you'd like to know my specific recommendations right now, just send me an email :)

Now, let's move on to the fourth way to maximize the ROI of all of your visitors to your websites, *ENTRY pop ups*.

WATCH THE PREVIOUSLY-UNRELEASED VIDEO "How to Access a VIRTUALLY UNLIMITED Database of Your IDEAL Customers"!

Just forward a copy of your order receipt email (*from Amazon or Barnes & Nobles*) to bookbonus@ecommercesiteowners.com.

When we receive your receipt, we'll send you an email with the webpage to access your FREE gifts!

CHAPTER 5: ENTRY POP-UPS

"Give Them A Good Reason To Share Their Contact Information"

The next marketing technique that we can use to maximize our profits from every single visitor to our site is through the use of ENTRY Pop Ups.

Now, this technique is similar to the previous one that we just covered, however the psychology behind why we use these (vs. EXIT pop ups) is different.

Now, you might be saying again "Mark, I hate those type windows and I don't want to put those on my website because it irritates my customers."

Then Mark will say "I agree. I don't like popups either, but the proven fact is that they work."

That's why we continue to use them.

They build our list and generate new sales automatically.

Basically, Entry pop-ups are **unblockable pop-ups that appear when you're initially visiting a site** (or when you're coming back to visit a site again).

Again, the idea is to get the first sale and/or interaction with a customer, and your goal is to keep them from leaving "empty-handed", or from giving you their contact information.

When you have their contact information, it provides you an opportunity to build a relationship with them, what typically happens on my eCommerce sites, where they visit once and never come back again.

Best Practices for Implementation

As the technology has evolved, there have been many new and interesting ways to implement these type popups on your site, in a way that doesn't "bug" your visitors.

For example, you can set it so that it only pops up after someone has been on the site for 30 seconds, 2 minutes, or whatever timeframe you want.

In addition, you can set it up where it only pops up after they've viewed at least two / five / ten pages, so they've taken action to show you that they're interested in going deeper into your site and learning more about your products.

You can also set it up to where the popups don't show up more than once every seven days, for example, so it doesn't show every single time, just on the schedule you decide.

Another option is that can set it up where, if you've ALREADY captured their contact information, then you don't show the pop-up to that customer again, since they've completed the action that you wanted them to complete.

Also, you do not have to ONLY show the popups on the homepage of your online store.

You can actually use them to **show a special offer** *related to visiting a specific page or product.*

Many times, that's an ideal solution so that you have certain pop-ups that only appear on certain product or category pages, and then you can really fine-tune your message and offer to best fit exactly what you're wanting them to purchase.

Offer Ideas To Get Started

As you get started, you can simply implement one or more of these "typical" offers that have been shown to work well.

The most simplistic offer is to just do a certain **dollar amount or percentage off** the purchase. 50% off works great, if you can afford it.

In addition, you can offer **free shipping** through usage of a coupon code that you give them.

INSIDER'S TIP: Don't ever, EVER just give your prospects "free shipping" without forcing them to take some sort of an action, on their part. We want to force them to actually do something (i.e. show they're serious) and at least opt in to get information for their free shipping code. In addition, we require that they actually INPUT that code into the check-out process. Again, that tells us that they're serious, and that they are action takers.

Consider This...

When you simply make it where ALL customers get free shipping, and its automatically setup that way in the shopping cart, they don't value what you're doing for them.

They didn't have to work for it or do ANYTHING, so they don't appreciate your gift, and they're probably not going to be great long-term customers.

In essence, you're literally HANDING THEM money out of your pockets to pay for their shipping, and not getting any benefit back, so just DON'T DO IT!

Make them work for it... Just a little.

Few More Ideas

One additional idea to include in your entry pop ups is that you could do the "time-tested" join my newsletter or coupon club type offer.

You may find that many people, in your target demographic, will respond positively to that type offer, however again, you'll want be capturing their email address, at the minimum.

Ideally, you can also capture their mobile phone number and mailing address to give you more follow-up options in the future.

Obviously, the more information that you can get, the better, however, many people are finding that that email marketing is getting less and less effective in certain markets.

INSIDER'S TIP: *The Internet's spam filters are catching even legitimate messages, and many times you will see that even 50% (or more) of all the people who you send your emails to, aren't actually getting them, because they are being filtered out - either through Gmail, or your email hosting provider, or the recipient's hosting provider, or the internet provider, like a Comcast or Cox, etc.*

A huge benefit with having your customers' mobile phone numbers, is that you can set up automated text campaigns to provide them with additional information or give them special offers.

These type marketing messages have been shown to work extremely well because people always look at or respond to text messages that show up on their phone, because its *always by their side.*

Think about what items are most important for you to never leave home without...

Most people say its their keys, their wallet/purse, and their phone.

Take advantage of that fact, and use it to build a deeper relationship with your customers

Next, having a full mailing address for your customers give you the ability to send direct mail, flyers, postcards, sales letters, and special offers.

Again, when you undertake a direct mail campaign, take the time to really assess your customer group, their interests, their age range, their gender, where they live, their hobbies, etc.

In many cases, you'll find that sending them something in the mail can be SIGNIFICANTLY more profitable that any email campaign that you ever do.

The reason being that some markets respond much better to direct mail / having a physical "something" in their hand, that they can read VS. having to read another marketing email, which they're already bombarded with on a daily basis.

Again, when you're gathering your prospects contact information using Entry pop ups, the same rules apply.

Start off by just collecting email addresses, and then take them to a secondary page where you then collect more detailed information like first name, last name, mobile phone number, mailing address, and possibly some additional information about their interests.

Again, all you are looking for with these entry pop-up types of marketing programs is to *build long-term relationships*.

INSIDER'S TIP: If you have a way to contact them, you can have the opportunity to tell them your story, build rapport, and differentiate you and your business from your competitors.

Don't Be Just Like Everybody Else

One of the biggest failures of most business owners, is that they don't place a HUGE emphasis on differentiating their company/their products from all of their competitors.

Let me be clear…

There is NOTHING more important than differentiating yourself from your competitors.

If you're products are markedly different (and better) than your competitors' products, then you are selling a "commodity", where the most important buying decision for a customer can only be "where can I buy this for the cheapest price".

You can't win at this game.

A larger, more financially "deep-pocketed" company can always come in and beat you immediately on price because they have a lot more money and they can buy alot more product from the manufacturer, in bulk.

In fact, some of the leading big-box retailers will even sell the product at a loss, just to dominate and take over the market.

For example, just look at Amazon.com. They make billions of dollars in revenue (i.e. not profit) a year, *but are still losing money*.

Companies like this are playing the "long term" game, aren't worried about immediate profits, and want to become the dominate player in the market so they can use that built-in list of customers to promote other, more profitable products, in the future.

You're not Amazon, and unless you want to go out of business very quickly, don't play that game.

Competing only on price is a losing proposition. Differentiation fixes that problem immediately because (in the customers mind, at least), your product is unique / it provides them with additional benefits that other competing products do not, and your premium pricing reflects that uniqueness.

Easy Ways to Make Your Product Different / Better

Once again, if you have a product that's no different from any of your competitors, then stop selling that product.

You have to make it different.

I'll share some of the different ways that we strategically-position our products to avoid competing on price and being seen as a commodity to our prospective customers.

First, if the product is proudly "**Made-in-the-USA**", that can be a huge benefit that we love to promote, and utilize in all of our marketing.

Many people that we come into contact with (primarily US based consumers) will resonate with that sentiment, and are very proud of keeping jobs / making products in the United States.

That being said, if you're not based out of / sell into the United States, this idea can absolutely be applied ANYWHERE else in the world, by just making a simple change in the marketing to say "Made in Canada", "Made in Germany", "Made in Italy", etc.

A second way to differentiate your company and its products is to let people know that you are a **small, family-owned business**, *if that in fact is a true statement.*

In our businesses, we truly do operate as a "small, family-owned business", *in every way possible.*

<u>We're not a big nameless, faceless corporation.</u>

You can see the faces of people who work for my companies on our websites.

You can see our phone number and we actually answer the phone.

In my opinion, I think people want to do business with other people who are similar to them, and that they *know, like, and trust.*

As such, if you can help them to understand that you are like them and care about them (which you do), they'll be more likely to support you.

INSIDER'S TIP: By the way, did you know that the United States Small Business Association recognizes a "small business" to be defined as "organizations with less than $50 million in annual revenue". So yep... I'm DEFINITELY a SMALL business owner.

In addition, I can tell you that building a strong differentiation for your company and its products can justify a price that's significantly higher than any of your competitors.

Even if the actual product that you're selling, is IDENTICAL to your competitors' lower priced versions.

For example, I can tell you from personal experience that we have products that sell all-day-long, and twice on Sundays, for a SIGNIFICANT premium over our competitors, for no other reason than the story that we're better able to tell about our company, our brand, our products, and our customer service experience.

Why Build a List of Prospects In the First Place?

When you actively use marketing techniques like Entry Popups, and other list building activities to capture the contact information of your prospects and customers, you are building a valuable asset for your business.

Promotions to House List

For example, you can include these people in your long-term **"house list"** for future promotions, special sales, special discounts, and special mailing list-only offers that you don't publish on your own website.

Keep in mind that these "prospects" are valuable people to have on your list. Maybe they are not ready to buy currently, however they may be interested in buying in the future.

After all, they've already raised their hand and said they are interested in being learning more about you and your business in the first place, so take advantage of that relationship and include them in future marketing campaigns.

Education-based Selling

Next, you can focus on building your relationship with the customer by just providing them with valuable education & training that relates to the types of products you're offering, and providing them with additional ways to stay in touch.

As I mentioned before, some people like to engage on Facebook, some on Twitter, some on YouTube, and some by podcast.

Provide your customers with multiple ways to learn more about you, engage with you, and become part of the community through these follow up campaigns.

For example, you can actually develop education-based follow-up sequences that last a year or two, just to make sure that you're "right there", when they're ready to buy.

Constantly try to re-engage with your customers and let them know *why they should do business with you*, and *why they should do it now*.

Hopefully you'll build that relationship to where they become good, long-term customers that refer new businesses to you over time.

Creative Selling Psychology Through Email

Now let's talk about the importance of the **follow up email sequence**.

First of all, you can again provide helpful information related to your products and their "most beneficial" usage. For example, how to best use your particular product to do what they are looking to do. *That's always a great angle to use in your promotions.*

In addition, one of the most powerful ways that you can use your follow-up system to build trust and rapport + stimulate sales, is to make different "sales presentations" or "sales angles" that appeal to different people.

Before going into these psychological triggers that you should include in your marketing, at the very least, you want to set a deadline for them to take action and to make sure to follow up with your prospects, multiple times, over a 7-day period so that they they take action and actually complete the purchase.

That's the most important thing.

Now, with that being said, there are three distinct psychological marketing techniques that we try to utilize in our sales process.

The first of which is to speak to the **LOGICAL benefits** of the product.

For example, let them know logically why your product will help them or get them closer to their goals. One way of saying this might be to say that your product *"will save your time and money, by making it easier to do X, without have to do Y."*

Its "fact-based" selling where you're just telling them about the benefits of *your* products versus other leading products. This often works extremely well.

The next technique that you can utilize, if the logical angle doesn't generate a sale, is to develop another sales message that focuses more on the **FINANCIAL benefits** of a particular product. For example, *"It's the best price you'll find, special offer only available for the next 48 hours, cheaper than competing products, time saving benefits, money saving benefits, etc."*

You already know that you never want to compete on price. However, what we are doing is juxtaposing our current price, the price that we have publicly visible on the website, with this new or better, cheaper price that we are offering to them since they took that next step, and opted in.

INSIDER'S TIP: In this step, you want to basically talk to the "bargain-lover" characteristic of all people, so they'll know that they're getting a good deal.

Finally, if that doesn't work, then you'll want to speak about the **EMOTIONAL benefits** of your products. For example, *"Get this so you can impress your neighbors, or so you can spend more time with your family. Think about how that will feel, so you can get the recognition you deserve."*

Whatever speaks personally to the emotional benefits that someone would get from use of your products is a great way to help them to understand the importance of purchasing that product right now.

How Your Emails Should Look... for Maximum "Trust ability"

When running a small business and trying to relate on a more personal level with your customers, projecting a more *personal* look-and-feel vs. a more *corporate-y, sales-y polished* look, has been a successful technique for our own businesses, and its one that I recommend.

Now, you might be saying, *"Well, I want to look super professional."*

I understand completely. Here's the deal.

Your prospects' "BS-detector" is very high, at all times, and they are typically very suspect of very professional, sales-y, and polished marketing collateral.

The angle that I've always found success with is that you want to promote the fact that you are just a *regular person* out there, who has a small family business, and that <u>YOU ARE REAL</u>.

People like to do business with people that are real, and that they relate to.

One way to promote your being a "real" person vs. a big corporation, through email, is by using a plain and simple, *text only* look. By that I mean, just a simple text-based email, without a header graphic, a footer, and all these fancy graphics and flash.

We also try to use very colloquial *(i.e. informal, like a friend would talk to one another)* expressions, vs. what a big corporation would use: "Dear Mr. Customer, We've been in business since 1942, and we have over 100,000 employees with offices in all 50 states."

We don't communicate like that. We'll say something like, "Hey John, this is Mark from XYZ website. We've just received your order, and we really appreciate your business. We'll be shipping out your products this afternoon and will send your tracking number as soon as we have it. If we can ever help you, just let us know." \

In addition, as we've talked about previously, we always try to use actual names and faces of our employees, so they know there are actual people behind the company. *Always avoid sales-y or "slick" language.*

INSIDER'S TIP: *Here's one quick tip. If you've ever received a message or sent a message from your iPhone or iPad, it puts a little note at the bottom of the email message that says, "sent from iPhone" or "sent from iPad".*

Use that idea in your email marketing, so that looks like it's actually personally sent from the people, <u>even though it might be an auto responder</u>.

It looks more real and personal, and like the person actually responded and sent that email from their personal iPhone or iPad. That builds the concept that real people are behind this site, and their business is tremendously importantly.

In addition, you'll always want to use deadlines on every single offer that you make, and then send your follow up messages at <u>optimal times for consumption</u>.

For example, you can do a search online to see the current research data for the most popular days/times for everything. For example, for email opens vs. Facebook vs. Twitter vs. Youtube vs. Pinterest, etc.

Look at the optimal times for consumption, and then just schedule those messages to go out at those times where your people are most apt to actually read and take action.

No, No, No on Checkout Pages

Omit ANY type of pop-ups on shopping cart and checkout pages because it may confuse a person and it might take them away from the actual checkout page.

There's nothing worse than being on the checkout page, and they're ready to buy, when a pop-up appears up to say, *"Get 20 dollars off this order by entering your email here."*

All of a sudden, they are taken away from the checkout page, they've lost focus, and maybe they don't get the email that you sent out. They never come back to your site and order, or every time that they come back they are going to be <u>expecting a special offer</u> to actually finish that checkout. So, be very careful in that, and omit those pop-ups from your cart and checkout pages.

Timelines for Followup

Finally, when you're looking to build a long-term customer relationship building sales process, you'll want to follow up multiple times via email, text, and phone over a 90-day period.

You are not following up every day, but every few days you want to touch base, and it might be very informal. For example, just asking, *"Are you still interested in the product XYZ?"* And that's it.

INSIDER'S TIP: We've found that simply allowing them to <u>reply directly to you</u> can get a tremendous response, so definitely try it.

Over a 90-day period, you will basically be able to tell your story and hopefully get them interested in your company/brand/product, so keep it light and interesting, not sales-y, and you'll do well.

Once again, I'm not noting specific apps, because we change which ones we like all the time, because there's new ones coming out all the time that do a little bit better job for less money. You can very easily research that for whatever shopping cart you use, however if you'd like to know my specific recommendations right now, just send me an email :)

Now, let's move on to the fifth way to maximize the ROI of all of your visitors to your websites, *Facebook and Twitter Retargeting*.

GET INSTANT ACCESS TO THE 13 PART VIDEO TRAINING PROGRAM THAT MARK DEVELOPED TO ACCOMPANY THIS BOOK!

Just forward a copy of your order receipt email (*from Amazon or Barnes & Nobles*) to bookbonus@ecommercesiteowners.com.

When we receive your receipt, we'll send you an email with the webpage to access your FREE gifts!

CHAPTER 6: FACEBOOK AND TWITTER RE-TARGETING

"Remember Me? CLICK HERE to Complete Your Order!"

Retargeting your advertising keeps your company in the mind of the consumer. It is a way to grab a customer who has bounced, a term used for someone who visits a website, yet does not purchase, and encourage them to return to make a purchase.

Research indicates that only *2 percent of customers who visit a website the first time make a purchase*, while *retargeting allows the company to reach 98 percent* of those who bounced.

How it Works

Using cookies and a JavaScript code, retargeting enables you to basically follow those bounced customers as they travel throughout the Internet. The small code, which is placed on your website, is unnoticeable to visitors and does not affect the performance of the site.

Each time a new visitor arrives on the website, an anonymous cookie is dropped on the user, so that when the visitor travels throughout the web with that cookie, the retargeting provider is triggered to show them your advertisements on other web pages.

Retargeting Statistics

The statistics regarding the efficiency of retargeting are staggering. According to an article on CMO.com, nearly three out of five buyers in the United States say that they notice advertisements for products they look up on other sites, and 30 percent of consumers view targeted ads positively.

One of the most surprising statistics, however, was that retargeting could boost ad response by 400 percent.

In addition, 25 percent of those surveyed said that they enjoyed receiving targeted ads because they reminded them of items they were seeking previously.

Also consider that the average click-through for display ads is 0.07 percent, the click-through for retargeted ads is 0.7 percent, and retargeted visitors are 70 percent more likely to convert.

Clearly it's easy to see that retargeting is a beneficial way to build sales.

Using the Social Media Giants to Convert Your Customers

Now that you understand what re-targeting is, in a general sense, we'll be discussing one of the most powerful ways to quickly implement retargeting in your online marketing plan.

Facebook and Twitter are two of the larger social media websites that allow you to re-target their users, with your products, on their platforms.

Each site allows you to actually build *"custom web audiences"* that you can then re-market to, on their platforms, for very reasonable prices.

To get started, you can build your very own custom web audiences by simply copy and pasting HTML/Javascript code into your sites.

The script basically adds a tracking cookie each visitor's computer, so you can market to them through re-targeting later on.

Why Retargeting on Facebook and Twitter?

The idea behind retargeting is that once someone comes to your website or a web page, the retargeting pixel is added to your prospects computer, and you then have the ability to market to them on additional platforms.

These are extremely valuable leads because they've already been to your website and initially seen what you have to offer, so they have some knowledge of your website and its products.

<u>Re-targeting also gives you the ability to test different types of offers.</u>

For example, when they originally came to the website for the first time, maybe they didn't particularly like the offer that was being made on a product.

Maybe they didn't take the time to go deeper into your site.

What Offers to Make

By implementing re-targeting marketing, on two of the world's largest social platforms, you can actually build on that recognition that they already have of your brand, and present them with different types of offers.

- You could offer them *free shipping* for them to come back and purchase.

- You could offer a certain *dollar amount* or *percentage off* their total order.

- You could offer *limited-time sales*, like 25% off for Labor Day or whatever it might be.

- You could also offer *free downloads and gifts*. For example, maybe they're not ready to actually buy. Maybe they need some time to "think about it" and become more educated on the benefits of your product and what it will do for them to make their life better.

- You could also offer *contests and giveaways* which are always a great way to get your prospects interest *(and hopefully their contact information for future follow-up)*.

- You could also offer different *product variations, sizes, colors, and bundles*. For example, maybe they came to your site, and they wanted a *black* shirt - but maybe all you had was a *red* shirt.

Now you have the black shirt available, but *they just don't know about it.*

INSIDER'S TIP: For example, you could put together an ad that is "product specific" that says, "Hey, we see that you liked this product, but did you know that we also make a black version of this?" Or, "We make a 'platinum' version of this, and this is why you need it."

That's another great way, *without being too creepy*, to pique their interest enough to get them to come back to the site and, at least, give you their email address so you can follow up with them over time.

Another benefit of re-targeting is that you can usually <u>remove the customers</u> who have <u>already ordered</u> from the customer audience *so you're not wasting your money re-targeting customers who have already purchased.*

Because once they've purchased, you have their contact information, and then you can market to them in the future. You don't need to advertise to them to get that first order thereafter, and you can actually set it up so that when they come back to the site they won't be re-added to that customer audience.

Retargeting Options

In addition to setting up *"site-wide"* campaigns, you can also setup *category,* or *product-specific* campaigns, which can be tremendously powerful because you're really narrowing down <u>exactly what specific offer would make this person take the next step and purchase this specific product</u>?

What are the specific benefits of this product? What are the different marketing angles that we can address? Develop a focused retargeting program for this product so it makes it more interesting to the person coming back to your site.

In addition, when your prospects are on Facebook and Twitter, many times their "guards are down" a little bit, for lack of a better word.

They are busy being *social*, so in many cases they can be more open to some of your messages about how this particular product can help them.

INSIDER'S TIP: Now, one major negative with strictly retargeting ONLY on these platforms is that they <u>only target people with active Facebook or Twitter accounts</u>. And not only that, they need to be fairly active on those different platforms for you to really get much exposure to them.

So if you have a demographic that's super active on Facebook or Twitter, then this is a great option. However, you need to consider the characteristics of your prospective target market to know whether or not that's going to be effective.

Really the best way to find this out is to just try it. If you set up your retargeting campaign and you spend $50 on ads, and you don't get any clicks or exposures, it's not a big loss.

Honestly, I wouldn't quit after trying one ad, one time. I would definitely try new creatives with your ads. Possibly more granular targeting. And even trying out a new/different retargeting platform, altogether, that has a different inventory of available websites.

There is No Privacy On the Internet

Facebook and Twitter has one of the most extensive and detailed databases of customer demographics and activities in the world.

With that data, you're able to fine tune your re-targeting ads to more closely fit your exact "ideal customer" while keeping your advertising costs low.

For example, within the custom web audience group that you have, you can take it a step further.

You can say, not only do I ONLY want to target people who have actually visited my site, but I want to narrow it down any further to only target women, between the ages of 45 to 55, that live in Mississippi, Louisiana, Texas, are married, and have kids under 12.

That's the power of re-targeting.

You can find out more information on retargeting at Facebook.com/ads and ads.twitter.com right now.

Now, let's move on to the sixth way to maximize the ROI of all of your visitors to your websites, *web retargeting*.

LEAVE YOUR REVIEW FOR THE MAXIMUM PROFITS BOOK ON AMAZON.COM AT

www.ecommercesiteowners.com/addreview

As an additional bonus, when you do, just let us know by sending an email to support@ecommercesiteowners.com and we'll send you a private link to access my entire "How to Choose a Fun & Profitable Niche Market" course for FREE :).

CHAPTER 7: WEB RETARGETING

"Did I Just See Your Company Advertising On The Homepage of CNN.com?"

The year is 1984, and I'm in fourth grade at Dixie Elementary school in Hattiesburg, Mississippi.

Our teacher had given us an assignment to make our own book... come up with a story AND illustrate it.

Well, to this day, I've never been much of an artist. My hand writing is sloppy, and I even write all of my letters backwards. You see, I'm right handed but my first grade teacher was left handed, so I mistakenly learned to write my letters like a left-handed person by mimicking her writing a little too closely :)

Anyway, I busted my butt to put together the best little book, with the most creative story, and the most beautiful illustrations.

Or so I thought...

I turn it in and a few days later, my teach comes up to me after class and tells me:

"Mark, I just think it was so clever of you to make your book look like a kindergartener drew the pictures. That was very creative, and I'm really proud that you put so much thought into the simplicity of your illustrations. I'm choosing yours to be the winner of our contest and will be putting your book up on our award board for everyone to see!"

Well, needless to say, I didn't INTEND for the pictures to look like a kindergartener drew them.

I had just worked hard and was just doing the absolute best that I could, with the limited drawing skills and talents that I had.

As a result, good things happened. Maybe even some things that I didn't deserve.

The point being that when you are committed to doing your best, and you work hard, consistently committed to achieving a goal... like building a fun & profitable eCommerce business... *good things WILL happen to you.*

You WILL eventually have success because the world rewards action takers.

With web-retargeting you're taking an important action by capitalizing on your previous investments in PPC, SEO, video marketing, and all other lead generation activities that you've been actively running to get visitors to your online store.

You're able to then "retarget" that group of visitors, all over the web, on tens of thousands of different sites.

Keep in mind that these people have already been to your site and expressed interested in what you sell.

The timing just might not have been right for them, or they got distracted so they didn't make the purchase on that first visit.

With a well-designed web retargeting strategy, you can "stay in front" of them, across the sites that they visit on the web, and make it very easy for them to find your store and come back and buy when they ARE ready.

Now this is very similar to what we spoke about earlier on Facebook and Twitter re-targeting, however this takes it a step further.

You're not just re-targeting on Facebook and Twitter on their platforms - you're able to actually re-target all over the web.

For example, if you're familiar with large, high traffic sites like nbcnews.com or amazon.com or cnn.com, you can actually re-target your ads on those sites.

In addition, there are probably millions of other sites that are very *specifically-focused around topics that your target demographic and your customer would be interested in*.

Web retargeting is a great way to, very cost effectively, get in front of them once again, and remind them that they came to your website, they were interested in this product, and that they need to come back and buy now.

With web re-targeting (vs retargeting on Facebook and Twitter), we're **building what we call re-targeting lists** by pasting code into our site.

Now again, many times you can just paste this re-targeting code into the admin area of your shopping cart. But sometimes you have to get in and actually paste it into the actual HTML files, which is not difficult at all.

However, if you're not comfortable doing that, you can hire somebody to do it very, very inexpensively - and typically your host will even do that for you.

In addition, at the current time, it's very inexpensive to re-target your audience across the web on the different retargeting platforms.

Differences Among Retargeting Platforms/Providers

There are many different web retargeting platforms and/or providers, and each of them have a <u>different inventory of partner sites that they show advertisements on</u>.

Some providers' networks are more niche market focused. For example, certain platforms may be better for dog lovers, for fans of Jiu Jitsu, or whatever it might be.

As such, there are different retargeting services that work better for different markets and for a different type of target prospects that you're trying to find.

Now, these customers are some of your best prospects, because they've already expressed interest in either your brand, or your company, or your website, or in specific products.

That's great because it means they can be pre-disposed to be more responsive to your ads and offers.

Types of Offers

With web retargeting providing many of the same benefits as Facebook / Twitter retargeting, you can similarly test different types of offers.

You may not know what offer will work best with a particular group, so you can test a few different offers through rotating banner advertisements.

For example, you might try be a **free shipping coupon offer, or a certain dollar amount or percentage off**.

INSIDER'S TIP: In our own experiences, we've found that both of these type offers can work extremely well, as does a <u>limited-time sale related to a special event or a holiday</u>.

In addition, free downloads or gifts that help you to better tell your story and differentiate your product from all others, are also great options.

You're sharing valuable education and helpful tools and resources to people, whether or not they buy from you. That's valuable to your customers, and it works really well.

You can also do **contests and giveaways**.

Now you may say, *"Well that's just a waste of time Mark. They're just interested in the free iPad that I'm giving away."* But you have to remember, in this scenario, we are only targeting people <u>who have already expressed interest</u> in your product, your website, your company, or your brand.

These are very qualified people, so if it takes some sort of a low-end giveaway or even a high-end one like an iPad, *many times you will find that it's worth it*, because of the viral nature of this kind of campaign.

You can also do **different product variations** or **sizes** or **bundles**. For example, they may have come to your site and found a black shirt that they like the *style of*, but they didn't like the *color*, and they didn't take the time to look around and really try to find the color that they were looking for.

A good opportunity for you might be to set up a *product specific* re-targeting campaign. You say, *"Hey, did you know that we offered this shirt in green?"* That might prompt their interest and encourage them to come back.

Think About What's Actually Going On in Your Customer's Mind

People are lazy by nature, and when they come to your site, more often than not, they don't follow the process (i.e. visit the product page, add to cart, checkout) exactly as you'd like them to.

They're busy and they come to your site and "poke around" on some different pages.

While that's occurring, at the same time, *they may have people screaming in their ear*, or a *million different distractions* going on.

***INSIDER'S TIP:** I can tell you right now, I have probably fifty tabs open in my browser. So I know how easy it is to get off topic, and get distracted, and life happens.*

Whenever you have an opportunity to get the attention of a previous visitor to your site, on other sites, at different times when they might be more receptive, that's a good thing.

Web retargeting offers that ability.

How to Get Started

Web re-targeting is a slightly more involved process to implement, but not much more so than what we used for setting up our Facebook & Twitter retargeting.

Again, it basically just involves the simple task of <u>adding the retargeting code on your website</u>, <u>collecting that list of people to re-target to</u>, and <u>setting up budgets</u>, <u>and designing different sized banner ads</u> with your creative message and call-to-action.

About Banner Graphics

Different partner websites on each of these sites allow for different-sized banners or graphics.

Some the most popular banner sizes are the 300 x 250 pixels wide and 728 x 90 pixels wide, so those are the two that you'll probably want to start out with, because most sites allow them.

However, we will typically design these two sizes at the beginning, and then we test the offers between these to see which ones are performing the best for us.

We then make a determination whether or not we want to invest the time or money in developing additional banner sizes to work with multiple new sites in the network, for increasing our exposure.

Also, just like on Facebook and Twitter, you can also remove customers who have already ordered from the retargeting list that you're advertising to, in most cases, by excluding the "order complete" page.

This aspect of web-retargeting provides you with the major benefit of saving your budget by not re-marketing to people who have already purchased.

INSIDER'S TIP: *You don't want someone who has just purchased a $100 waffle iron on your site to then go to nbcnews.com and see that you're offering the same waffle iron for 50% off when that was just intended for people who have never purchased before.*

Final Considerations

Again, one of the primary benefits of using this type of web re-targeting in your eCommerce marketing is that it allows for MUCH additional exposure across the web, and not just on Facebook or Twitter.

Before investing in either a Facebook/Twitter or web remarketing campaign, you want to consider the demographics of your target market, and determine if they ARE or are NOT active on Facebook and Twitter.

If they have their account on both of those platforms, but they're not active, *they are never going to see those ads in the first place.*

However, with WEB re-targeting, your ad will have much more exposure on thousands and thousands of sites vs. just Facebook and Twitter.

Wherever they go across the Internet, they'll be able see your ad, and that's why we typically start with web retargeting first.

That being said, the one negative with web retargeting is that there's not as much control over which sites your ads show up on, or the reporting of granular level detailed information on which sites that your ad is on and perform best.

For example, on most platforms, you can't say for , "Well, website abc123.com is really performing poorly, I want to turn that one off, and save my budget for better performing ones."

Conversely, you typically don't have the information you'd need to be able to say, "Website 12345.com is performing really well, so I want to up the percentage of my ad spend that goes to that site".

As such, that's a negative aspect of this type of advertising (on most retargeting platforms) as you're not able to see that type information. It's basically just auto-optimized by these providers.

Web retargeting is a great way to get in front of, and re-engage with those people who have expressed interest already, and have already visited your website without purchasing.

The retargeting platforms that we use, change over time, but at the time of this writing, a couple of services that we've used in the past include perfectaudience.com and sitescout.com.

I encourage you to check them out for yourself, checkout their reviews, and talk to people that have used them before to get their feedback.

Then just go out there and try them out, because **web re-targeting is one of the most incredibly efficient advertising methodologies that we've found**.

Now, let's move on to the seventh and final way to maximize the ROI of all of your visitors to your websites, *several "BONUS" Tips & Tricks from the eCommerce Pros.*

ACTIVATE YOUR FREE 30 DAY MEMBERSHIP TO THE ECOMMERCE SITE OWNERS.COM "PLATINUM ELITE" COACHING PROGRAM!

Just forward a copy of your order receipt email (*from Amazon or Barnes & Nobles*) to bookbonus@ecommercesiteowners.com.

When we receive your receipt, we'll send you an email with the webpage to access your FREE gifts!

CHAPTER 8: BONUS "TRICKS" FROM THE PROS

"Warning. Using the Marketing Techniques That You're About to Learn Can Cause You to DRASTICALLY Increase Your Sales :)"

In this section, we're going to be covering some really cool bonus tricks from the eCommerce pros. Now, these are marketing techniques that aren't well known by most online business owners, however, they're extremely powerful.

Don't underestimate how simple ideas can make positive changes to your profitability of your business, because **they've made a significant difference in the profitability of both our own, and our consulting clients' online stores.**

How To Make Money From Free Shipping

This is a really killer trick that we began using several years ago. Here's the big idea: You want to **always market your store as offering free shipping, but make your customers EARN it**.

This particular promotional concept is simple-to-understand and well-understood by your prospects.

Free shipping is what your customers have been conditioned to expect, in many markets, so you want to give them what they want.

You don't want to make it difficult for them to purchase from you, and you don't want them to even consider shipping cost as being a reason for not purchasing.

In certain cases, if they are expecting free (or very minimal) shipping, and you then add that shipping fee onto their shopping cart total, it may cause them not to purchase, as you're not meeting their expectations.

That being said, in most online stores that I do consulting with the owner on, I will recommend to always market your store as offering free shipping.

One aspect of this strategy that needs to be made clear is that, **you don't have to just give it away** to unqualified customers.

In reality, <u>you are giving them YOUR money</u> when you are taking the shipping fee out of <u>your</u> own profit margin, so *you get to make the rules.*

Since you get to make the rules, you can make your customers step through as many hurdles as you want because <u>you only want to deal with qualified customers</u> - *people who are serious, who are going to be good long-term customers.*

INSIDER'S TIP: You don't want people just looking for freebies coming to your site. You want them to have to take action and follow through, and do what they say they are going to do to in order to get the benefit of me giving them free shipping.

For example, on many of our sites, we ask our prospects *(who want to take advantage of the free shipping promotion)* <u>to take action</u> by providing us with their contact information through opting into a form with their email address or texting in.

Texting in to join my list / claim their free shipping code is, by far, my favorite method.

Basically you can say, "*Text your email address to 12345,*" Or, "*Text this short code to this phone number or short code, and then I will send you instructions on your free shipping coupon code to use when you're checking out.*"

You'll also want to make the free shipping offer <u>time sensitive</u>. For example, on our stores, we only make it valid *for 24 to 72* hours because I want them to take action IMMEDIATELY.

In addition, by joining our mailing list by SMS, we can make sure that our message gets through *(vs email),* and they get that code, since most people will typically have their phone right there by them at all times.

<u>It makes it very simple and convenient for them to complete their order, right now.</u>

Contrast that with email. Your customers are getting A LOT of emails on a daily basis, and when you send emails to them, their spam filters might incorrectly label your messages, so that they never even see your message.

We like to get their mobile phone number in our followup system, because its much more likely for them to see any messages we send in future marketing promotions.

Few Clarifications

The Number 1 rule is that you ALWAYS want to make the free shipping offer to be time-sensitive and make them DO SOMETHING in order to claim it.

In addition, you DON'T actually even need to have the free shipping code expire in your cart backend. *If that's a hassle, you can just change the code every so often.* I change it every month or so, so it's not always out there. But you just need to state that it's time sensitive, and give them a deadline.

Also, you want to *force them to manually input the coupon code during the checkout process,* versus just making it so that all products have 0% shipping *automatically*.

Many people ask, "*Why do you this? Why do you make this hard?*"

The reason is that **I want to PRE-QUALIFY people.**

I want people who are serious, that have a credit card, and are willing to do what I asked them to do to actually purchase products.

For example, *if they're just going to buy one time for me, I'm never going to make money,* and that's not the types of customers that I want to foster.

So I want to make sure that they can follow simple instructions, because I'm literally giving them $10, $20, or even more *out of my pocket*.

For them to just buy *one product…one time*, that doesn't help me. It actually makes me lose money, in many cases.

That's why we want to force them through all these steps to qualify themselves as a customer with whom I want to business.

INSIDER'S TIP: If possible, you want to build your shipping cost into the price of a product so your overall profitability isn't affected :) Whether or not they use the free shipping code, you really don't care because you've covered the cost of the shipping in your pricing.

Now, if you've not implemented the steps noted previously in this book, and your product is still considered a "commodity", you won't be able to do that, because they'll be able to easily compare that product among all the different competing products out there. And since you have shipping costs already built in, over and above your "normal" profit, then they will be able to go over to another site, and see that your pricing is significantly more.

That's why we never recommend selling a generic commodity type product. We always brand it and build a story around it. We tell why our product is better than other competitors'.

We never want to be competing strictly on price, and we never want to have a picture or a product description or a price allows them to easily compare our product with all the other ones on the Internet.

That's very, very important.

That way, we can build additional shipping costs into our sales prices *(because our products aren't easily comparable to other products out there, there's not an easy way to compare prices)*.

Whether or not they use the free shipping code, <u>it does not matter to us</u>, because <u>it's not affecting our overall profitability per product</u>.

Next, you want to **implement a follow-up system** to make sure that they take action over the period of promotion.

As I said, we typically do make the free shipping coupons "active" for 24-72 hours, and then we build in automated follow ups through text messaging, emails, and even personal phone calls.

Over that period of promotion, you don't want them to just have to remember on their own, <u>you want to constantly follow up with them</u>. Once a day is plenty, and then right before the deadline where the offer is expires.

INSIDER'S TIP: And here's the kicker. In my experience, 50% percent or more of all the customers who DO receive the free shipping coupon and DO order - do not end up using the coupon.

It doesn't make any sense; it's not logical. They have the coupon code right there on the mobile phone, in their text messages, or in their email. They've also likely talked to us via phone, or gotten a voicemail that reminds them about the coupon code.

<u>They still come and order, and they still don't end up using the coupon code.</u>

So lets recap what just happened.

- We've been able to advertise that we have free shipping, which is great.

- We've been able to have our prospects pre-qualify themselves as being serious customers.

- We've added them to our mailing list, so whether or not they buy, we can market to them in the future.

- We've also already covered ourselves as far as a profitability goes, so that we're not actually losing any money in giving them the free shipping.

- Finally, if they DO order, we'll actually even get to keep the actual shipping fee (that we'd already added into the "normal" price) as additional profit.

This technique works great, and you should use it immediately.

You're not being tricky or unscrupulous; you're being very upfront. And if any of our customers should ask why we make them jump through so many hoops to claim the free shipping code, I'll tell them - *"We do it this way because we want to qualify you as a customer."* And in almost all cases, they are okay with that. They understand that a business can't operate with a bunch of freebie seekers.

Use this "trick". It's one my favorite ones, and we implement it on almost every one of our stores. It's an opportunity for significant additional profits on top of what you're already doing.

Finally, you cover yourself from a profitability standpoint, you're able to market yourself as offering free shipping *(which is a differentiator from many of your other competitors)*, and it's just a great way to maximize a value from every single visitor that you have.

Pre-Populate Forms with Geo or Geographic IP Address Data

The basic idea of this technique is to make it as quick and easy as possible to order or to request information.

As a quick overview, an IP address is basically a computer's UNIQUE address on the Internet, and it can be used to decipher *(in most cases)* that particular computer's location.

For example, there is technology that will allow you to use that IP address *(of that person that's shopping on your site)* and you can usually determine their city, state, zip, and country.

Now, this is not 100% accurate all the time, however it works well, and this data will allow you to **pre-populate web forms (i.e. ORDER forms) with city, state, zip and country information**.

The pre-population of forms is good for everyone as it saves time for your *customers*, and it greatly increases YOUR conversions, because you've just pre-populated four different fields that they no longer need to fill out.

You can pre-populate an **order form**, or even just an **opt-in form** for your customers to claim a special gift or a promotion.

The more simple you can make every single process on your site, the more likely that people are going to be *to take advantage of your offers, to complete their orders*, or to raise their hand and say *"I'm interested in this, send it to me."*

The technology isn't perfect, but it works well enough to try out.

It can save you potential lost business from people who may not have taken the time to complete your order forms that, in their opinion, take too long to fill out.

People are always in a hurry, they've got a million things going on.

Make it as easy as possible for them to interact with you by pre-populating their forms with as much information as possible.

Personal Phone Calls with an Offer

The next insider's tip is to use personal phone calls to followup with your customers, after they place an order.

Now, you might ask, *"Why would I actually want pick up the phone and call someone after they've actually ordered?"*

The reason is because it provides a great customer experience, will build goodwill with your customers, and if done right, can increase your per order profits significantly.

Keep in mind that doesn't have to be you calling, either.

You can easily have these phone calls completed by an outsourced virtual assistant that you pay $8-$10 an hour, or even outsource to a part-time employee in the Philippines, for $2-$3 an hour, who can call the same 50-100 people in a day.

It doesn't matter which route you choose. Both work, and will make you additional profits.

My Proven Script

When we receive an order from one of our eCommerce stores, or our Amazon stores, or our eBay stores, or our Etsy stores, we will call every customer to ask a few very specific questions:

#1 - *Did you receive your product*? Yes or no.

#2 - *Was it what you expected?* Yes or no.

#3 - *Were there any aspects of the products that we could improve?* Now this is going to give you some great information, because you're going to get feedback from the customers on exactly *what they liked, what they didn't like, what they'd like to see,* so we can use that information to improve our products in the future.

The beauty of this technique is that you're not trying to "sell them" at all :)

INSIDER'S TIP: We are trying to build a relationship and let them know that we're a real business who cares about their needs, and wants to make sure that we're providing exactly what they need and want.

At the end of the short call, we simply say, *"Thanks very much. Would you mind if I emailed you special customer thank you coupon for $X dollars off you next order?"*

Of course, they'll say, *"Yes."*

Why Do This?

The personal followup phone call serves multiple purposes.

#1 - *It provides extraordinary customer service,* and *lets them know that you appreciate their business.*

#2 - *It starts off the entire business/customer relationship in a very positive way.* It also allows you to further differentiate your "small family business" from the big, monstrous corporations that would never think of picking up the phone and actually calling them.

#3 – Finally, depending on when you actually make the calls (*either immediately after the order is placed or after they've actually received the product),* it gives you a lot of valuable feedback on the quality of your products, your order fulfilment process, and helpful information to know if you're meeting/exceeding the expectations of your customers.

For example, *are they getting what they're expecting? How can we improve the product? What things do they like the most? What things do they like least?*

When we've completed the call, we then add their email address and other information into an automated followup sequence so that we automatically send over their coupon, and provide ongoing promotions to get them to come back to your OWN online store (where your profits are highest) and do more business down the road.

New Customer Follow Up System

One of the most profitable marketing campaigns that you can run is the "New Customer Followup System".

After someone buys from you, and you have proven that you provide the highest levels of customer service / they got more than they expected, these same customers are at the peak level of customer satisfaction, and <u>we want to capitalize on that fact.</u>

How to Generate Testimonials on Auto-Pilot

First of all, when we have their order information and we've called them, we can also build followup systems that include emails, text messages, and voice messages **to capture testimonials about our products on autopilot.**

If you been online for any length of time, you'll know that testimonials and reviews have become incredibly important and that *social proof is one the most important factors to help you to sell your product.*

Build your systems to automatically generate testimonials over time, on autopilot, and then <u>use those in your marketing</u>, *to increase your sales even more to new prospects.*

Get More Referrals… on Automatic

You can also generate referrals on autopilot when you integrate affiliate software into your store, which allow your customers to refer other people to your store at no cost!

Of course, you then only pay them when their referrals turn into a sale for your online store. There is no upfront cost *(other than the minimal cost of the affiliate software and initial setup)* and no risk to you.

Alternately, if you'd don't want to setup a formal affiliate program, you can just say in your emails something like *"Hey if you like your product, we're a small family business and one of the ways that we're able to make it is through referrals from happy customers just like yourself. If you happen to know of anyone that would be interested in product XYZ, we'd appreciate it if you'd send them a link right below this to check out our site."*

This idea is very simple, but rarely actually used because store owners don't realize its true potential.

In addition, this technique can allow you to generate "viral" sales as you get more and more customers who choose to share your website and its products through their personal networks and social media accounts.

Launch New Products, Sales, and Special Offers to Your Best Customers

Next, you can use the new customer followup campaign to *market the launch of new products, special sales and offers*.

These people have already purchased from you, you've called and spoken with them on the phone, and you've built a relationship.

They know what they can expect, they know you're listening, and they know that you're commited to reaching out to them on at least a monthly basis, and trying to serve their needs.

Another benefit of this powerful followup system is that it gives you a "built-in" database of people ready to provide you with an initial burst of sales and reviews, when you're ready to launch new products.

Finally, you can use the new customer followup system to, of course, build deeper relationships with your customers. As you know more about them *(and they know more about you)*, you can serve them better.

How to Capitalize on the e-Commerce Giants

The next technique that you can use to maximize your profits, is to **capitalize on the e-Commerce giants traffic and existing customer base.**

Three of the largest third-party platforms are Amazon, eBay and Etsy, and they each have huge amounts of "organic" traffic, which is basically just people who are already on their sites actively shopping.

One very important characteristic of these particular sites is that **they are made for people to come and BUY stuff.**

Someone who is on the amazon.com site, for example, isn't looking for the latest news, tips, articles, social media updates, or anything else.

They are looking to find (and buy) a product that solves their needs. Period.

These are people who have credit cards on file with each of the sites, typically, and we want to have our products available wherever people want ot buy them.

Whether that's on our OWN site, on amazon, on ebay, or anywhere else.

Make it easy and convenient for people to buy from you, and one way you can do this is to simply *set up your own shops on one or more of these platforms.*

I would recommend focusing on Amazon first, eBay second, and Etsy *(if you sell handmade products)* third.

What you're trying to do is acquire customers from these platforms, and get them over to your own eCommerce store for future sales and promotions.

Fast Start Formula

Start off by selling 1 to 5 unique products with MASS appeal.

You don't want to sell your entire product line out there, because it's going to take away from the sales on your own website.

You want these new prospects to buy at least one-time on your 3rd party stores, so you can then begin the process of building a relationship *(off of that platform, on your OWN website).*

Call them to confirm that they're happy with the transaction and the product. Offer them a coupon to join your mailing list. Let them know about your main eCommerce site and your other related products.

When you have built that initial relationship, then *you're going to transition them over to your own store*, where you can sell to them for a long period of time, at much higher profits.

Your goal is to acquire new customers at break even or even at a slight loss to introduce yourself and your online store.

Short-term profit isn't as important as the *lifetime customer value* where that initial sale can turn into a catalyst to generate new, long term future sales on our own online store.

Capitalize on the significant buying traffic that already exists on Amazon, eBay, and Etsy, as there are many people out there who ONLY shop on one or more of those three sites.

They do so because they trust those brands, and they trust that they're going to be taken care of well.

In addition, they know that if they buy through one of those familiar websites that they're going to get the products they ordered, and if they're not happy, they can return them, *quickly and easily.*

INSIDER'S TIP: Don't try to spend all your time and money doing PPC/SEO/Online Marketing to try get everyone to come to your own online store. That's never going happen.

Your store is never going to have as much authority Amazon or Ebay or Etsy.

If you know your target demographic is shopping on one of those three sites *(or any other site that allows you to sell your own products),* then take the time to open up a shop on one or more of these platforms and get your products in front of them.

Take advantage of that fact, simply go where the people are, and acquire those customers for future marketing.

Direct Mail

Direct mail is one of the most powerful, least understood, and most underutilized avertising mediums for eCommerce site owners.

We hear other business owners say things like, *"Direct mail doesn't work. I spent all this money on printing and postage. I took a lot of time to hand address these and write out letters and print them and put them in envelopes, and then I don't get a single sale! Its not worth the effort."*

<u>Just like everything in life, you've got to do it CORRECTLY, if you hope to see positive results.</u>

Most business owners do it wrong.

For example, when you have already built a relationship with the people that you're sending the direct mail to, and they already know your brand, it's a different story.

Especially when you're presenting an awesome offer.

You'll find that direct mail can work incredibly well.

Also if you're worried that everyone will immediately see your direct mail advertising as "junk" and throw it in the garbage without even reading it, *remember that your thoughts and feelings aren't necessarily the same as your customers.*

You may be a in a different age group, a different gender, live in a different part of the country *(or world)*, have had different experiences from your family and growing up, and/or having had specific negative experiences that have influenced your view on direct mail... *and its potential effectiveness.*

One of the major benefits of having mailing addresses for your prospects and customers is that you're able to send them postcards, letters, thank you notes, promotions, flyers, and more.

In some cases, certain customer groups that you target aren't as likely to click on a link in an email and go to your website and place an order.

The reason being that they might not prefer to use the computer or email. Maybe they prefer to receive a direct mail piece and call you to place their order over the phone.

<u>The reality is that you shouldn't care HOW they order, as long as they order.</u>

We have found that direct mail works extremely well in certain markets, and not as well in others.

The point is that you should definitely test it out and see how it works for you.

Direct Mail Ideas

Newsletters - One easy way to get started is to simply send out a monthly or quarterly newsletter to your existing list, and include offers. *The response can be extremely high.*

Postcards or short sales letters – These can work very well, depending on your specific offer and mailing list.

Handwritten "Thank You" Cards - *With every order, we send out hand written thank you cards.* You can have in-house staff do it, if you have bad handwriting, like I do.

We also use virtual assistants to send these out on autopilot. Every time there's an order, they get an email that says, *"Please send this message to this person."* They hand write it, stamp it, and put it in the mail.

Automated Greeting Cards

We also use a service called **sendoutcards.com**, where you can actually import an actual sample of your signature, and they have handwritten fonts where you can just type your message.

The font that's used actually looks like it's handwritten by a person, and they handle everything from the designs, to the printing, to the stamping, to the mailing.

At the current time, this service is very affordable to use, and best of all, you can even *send additional gifts with your cards like brownies and cookies.*

If you look at this from a customer's perspective, it's a pretty impressive customer service experience that they're likely to tell their friends about.

For example, you place an order, someone from that company immediately calls you back just to let you know that they received the order and that your business is appreciated.

Next, when the order ships, you get an email with the tracking number. Then a few days later, they get a handwritten thank you card in the mail, and maybe a couple of brownies, that just says, "Thank you for your business. If we can ever help you in the future, just let us know."

It's a very impressive presentation, and it will definitely make your company stand out in a positive way.

Letter Fulfillment Services

In an effort to outsource all of our direct mail printing and fulfillment, we also have used a service for sending out letters at *mailaletter.com*. They'll actually print out the letters, format them, put them in the envelopes, put a real stamp on it, and ship them out for you. All at a very affordable price.

If you're not doing direct mail, you're definitely missing the boat.

Don't just do it once, and always try a few different formats, like postcards, one-page sales letter, flyers, and other types to see what types of returns you get, and then build on any winners.

Inactive Customer "Reactivation"

Our final bonus trick from the pros is how to maximize the value of your "inactive" customers.

This technique is incredibly powerful, and if you've had a business for any length of time, you know that there are always some customers that buy once, and they go away.

They never come back, at all, or they take a year or more between reorders.

In either case, one of the easiest and most profitable sales that you can make is a new sale to an existing customer.

The reason being that there is no additional cost of customer acquisition and, since they've already purchased from you in the past, they already have some level of relationship with your company and its products.

You want your customers to come back more often and be "actively engaged" with your company.

What is an "Inactive" Customer?

Whether "active" customers are buying once a week, once a month, once a quarter, or once a year - whatever that might be to you, *you need to actively go out there and reactivate those previous customers.*

Many times, you'll find that these customers haven't gone way because of anything that you've done, *they've just forgotten about you.*

- *Maybe they haven't had the need for your types of products over that time period.*

- *Or maybe they don't know what OTHER types of products that you actually offer.*

- *Or maybe they need your product, right now, but just haven't had a reason to order now.*

You want to define what constitutes "inactive" to you and your business.

For example, does inactive mean all people who haven't ordered in three months? Six months? Or even twelve months?

It all depends, and there's no right answer. But you need to specifically define what that inactive criteria actually is, so that you can then pull that information out of your sales database for future marketing.

In addition, you'll want to take the time to confirm that you have up-to-date mailing addresses, names, phone numbers, and email addresses for these customers, so *as to minimize waste in your advertising budget.*

A Simple Customer Reactivation Campaign

There are many different ways to implement this type of a program, however we typically use a combination of email and direct mail.

Here is the basic structure of your campaign:

#1 - **Apologize for not being attentive to their needs and tell them that you've missed them**. You're truly sorry that you haven't been in touch with them, and you want them to come back.

#2 - **Make them a "no brainer", special offer**. We call it a "mafia offer"; it's an offer that they can't resist.

Put together a great product offer at a great price, that's not available anywhere else. Make them feel special. The idea is to give them something that is universally appealing that they will be crazy enough to take you up on.

#3 - **Make the offer time sensitive so they have to take action now**. Include a specific date and time when the offer is no longer valid.

In addition, there are several best practices that we've found to be helpful in developing this program.

- We will typically send a multiple direct mail pieces, which are followed up by corresponding emails that reinforce the availability of the offer and the time-sensitive nature.

- In addition, if we have access to their mobile phone number, then we also will typically integrate text message campaigns, voice broadcasts, and possibly even personal phone calls to, again, reinforce the offer and deadline

- If we're making outgoing phone calls, the script is very simple. We just let them know that we sent them a letter, ask if they have received it, tell them about the offer, tell them about the deadline, and attempt to close the sale over the phone.

- If they've NOT received the letter, we resend it (in PDF format) to them through email, just to make sure that they receive and know about the special offer and deadline

- The most important part of this entire campaign is to simply let them know *that we care about them* and *we want them back into our "family".*

INSIDER'S TIP: In most cases, its best to contact them through different methods just due to the fact that, some

people respond much better through text messaging, some through the phone, some through direct mail, and some through email.

Follow up *a minimum* of four to six times.

This isn't a strategy that you can just throw out there, and have immediate results. You need to follow up consistently and let them know that the deadline is approaching. Let them know the benefits to taking you up on the offer, and make it a no brainer.

Again, *the entire goal is to re-activate them into being an active customer who buys multiple items in the future.*

If they're "inactive", they are not thinking about you and they don't have you in the top of their minds, so they can't refer you to other people, and they aren't thinking about buying from you.

Remember that it's, almost always substantially cheaper…and more effective… to sell more stuff to EXISTING customers, than to acquire NEW customers.

> TO LEARN MORE ABOUT WORKING, ONE-ON-ONE, WITH MARK IN HIS PRIVATE ECOMMERCE COACHING PROGRAM, GO TO:
>
> WWW.ECOMMERCESITEOWNERS.COM/COACHING

CHAPTER 9: WHAT TO DO NEXT?

As we come to the end of this book, I want you to congratulate yourself for taking the initiative to #1 – buy this book in the first place, and #2 – actually READ the book *(and hopefully take massive action that makes a significant positive impact on your life).*

With your actions, you are now in the minority of all people, in that you actually take ACTION and make positive movement towards your goals.

That is definitely something to be commended, and I appreciate you're sharing your most valuable asset... *your time...* with me.

Hopefully, the tips, tricks, techniques, and creative marketing ideas that you've learned in this book will help you to make more sales.... *and* PROFITS... in your businesses, and help you to be more aware of the opportunities that are available to you in starting and growing your very own eCommerce store(s).

I can tell you that, this business is not difficult, however it DOES require hard-work, determination, perseverance, an open-mind, and a willingness to test new ideas, while also learning from your mistakes.

You have what it takes to be successful, and I believe in you.

After all, I'm just a small town farmboy from South Mississippi, and I was just like you. I didn't know anything about eCommerce when I got started, and <u>I had to learn by doing</u>.

I've invested *(and continue to invest)* tens-of-thousands of dollars in my own education, training, and ongoing expert mentorship so that I can be more successful in my own eCommerce businesses, while at the same time, using that knowledge to help my valued students inside the eCommerceSiteOwners.com "Platinum Elite" coaching program and through one-on-one consulting with serious business owners, just like yourself.

If you think that I might be able to be of service to you, send me an email at mark@ecommercesiteowners.com and let me know.

I, personally, answer each and every email that I receive, and I'd love to hear about your business.

So with that, I wish all of God's blessings on you and your family, and I look forward to seeing you on the inside of eCommerceSiteOwners.com!

Have a blessed day, and thanks for your business…

Mark Mattix

Can You Please Do Me A Small Favor???

If you liked this book, I would REALLY appreciate your leaving me a star rating and review on my Amazon page by going to:

http://www.eCommerceSiteOwners.com/addreview

p.s. After you add your review, send me an email at support@eCommerceSiteOwners.com and I'll send you a private link to access my entire "How to Choose a Fun & Profitable Niche Market" course for FREE :)

About the Author

Mark Mathis is a #1 Amazon best selling author, successful entrepreneur, eCommerce expert, and publisher of the top-rated eCommerceSiteOwners.com "Platinum Elite" Coaching Program.

Over the last 20 years, Mark has started, operated, and sold dozens of online stores & businesses in a wide variety of niche markets.

In addition, through his advanced training and education programs, he has been able to help hundreds of small business owners to recognize *(and exploit)* the power of the Internet, eCommerce & creative merchandising/retailing systems to grow their business profits exponentially through unique & time-tested marketing systems.

He is also the founder of Local Marketing Labs, which is one of the leading marketing agencies in the Southeastern United States, providing eCommerce, lead generation, internet marketing, & consulting services to successful business owners in a wide variety of industries.

Mark earned his Bachelors of Science degree in Real Estate & Finance from the University of Southern Mississippi, and his M.B.A. in Marketing/MIS from the Louisiana State University.

After graduation, Mr. Mathis worked with the global technology consultancy, Accenture, as a Strategy/Technology Consultant, where he worked with dozens of Fortune 500 and "startup" companies, in the design and build of complex computer systems including everything from corporate risk management systems to geographical information systems for oil exploration to online eCommerce portals for major energy companies.

Mark then went on to work as the marketing director for one of the largest data centers in the Southeastern United States, where he helped to grow the company's revenues, four-fold, in less than four short years, through the implementation of his creative marketing systems and techniques.

On a personal note, Mark is a Christian and lives in Baton Rouge, Louisiana, where he is happily married with three small boys. He also enjoys Led Zeppelin, basketball, baseball riding 4 wheelers, playing guitar, USM/LSU sports, and doing basically anything outside.

Mark can be reached by email at mark@eCommerceSiteOwners.com , or by phone at 225-910-6148 and has limited availability for one-on-one consulting and speaking engagements.

Look What Other Successful Business Owners, Just Like You, Are Saying About Mark…

"Mark has put together a fantastic step-by-step course based on his own phenomenal success having set up multiple dozens of successful eCommerce sites on his own. He's got it down to a science and I'm excited about this business model! I fully endorse this course…"

- Jim Cockrum, The Most Trusted Marketer Online
OfflineBiz.com / MySilentTeam.com

"As a 68 year old making my 1st entry into eCommerce, I had concerns that it would be a difficult project.
Thanks to Mark, it went smoothly. No geek talk, complicated instructions or anything like that. Mark built the site and I supplied product and pricing information. Now I have a great looking site and a new way to build my business."

- William Kloss
Pensacola, Florida

"Mark has done a fantastic job in chunking down for me the process of building out an eCommerce store into actionable steps and keeping me focused along the way. I'd urge anybody wanting to make a success out of their venture to follow Mark's formula."

- Stephen Sculfor
London, England

"I had been looking for so many answers to an e-commerce business that I was looking into and Mark was the right person. He is smart, insightful and knows this business inside and out."

Hampton L.

"The information is very useful for people who are starting a new business and need clear, step by step guidance on almost every aspect of getting an eCommerce store up and running in a short amount of time."

- Tom Shivers
Capture Commerce

"Wow, what can I say… I am COMPLETELY blown away! There is a wealth of knowledge in this course. So much in fact, that I find myself replaying the videos and uncovering another gem of information. What a great job!"

- Julio Felician
eCommerce Store Owner

"Our rankings on Google and other search engines, are number 1 or in the top 3, for every single category that we are in, we are now consistently growing our company's exposure on Facebook, Twitter, Youtube, and Google +, and most importantly, we are receiving significantly more calls from people finding our company on the Internet."

- Shawn Folks
Baton Rouge, Louisiana

"I knew from experience that finding someone to help me to create a quality website wouldn't be easy. Just maintaining a web presence with search engines such as Google, Yahoo, and Bing could be a full time job.
Mark Mathis is that guy."

- Christian Downward
Sterling, Virginia

"We have seen a significant increase in our internet leads. If you need more presence on the web, don't hesitate to give Mark your business. He is very easy to work with, and I recommend him highly."

- Jeremy Leake
Baton Rouge, Louisiana

"I have been online marketing for several years studying various courses and books. I came across Mark's book and purchased it. The book is a good guide to everything that you need to get out there and market your self and your company online in today's fast paced internet world."

- Chuck Walker
Atlanta, Georgia

"Mark took a look at our "homemade" web page several months ago. He described to us the opportunities for improvement and enhancement that would compliment our business.

Mark designed a new website with features that allowed our private practice an opportunity to reach new families who may be in need of our pediatric speech therapy services as well as enhance the quality of communication with our current families.

Mark's knowledge, attention to details, and creativity have allowed our staff to focus on our own strengths – providing quality speech-language therapy to children. He provided excellent online tutorials to walk us through the steps of managing certain aspects of our website on our own. We were truly impressed with his innovative ideas.

Within three months of Mark's services, we have already begun to see an increase in inquiries about our services through the website and find that our clinic name is on the first page of Google now when people search online.

Mark currently provides ongoing support that we are confident will continue to connect our clinic with the families of children for whom we can help reach their full potential."

- Sheran Samuel Benton, M.A., CCC-SLP
Baton Rouge, Louisiana

"In this day and age, dealing with so-called internet marketing experts and gurus is or can be a gamble because I have hired many and usually I end up losing money or disappointed. That's the risk you take in business.

However, I was either lucky or blessed when I found Mark. He has helped our company grow, exponentially, when he recommended to me and implemented a comprehensive and automated follow-up system that closed more new business than ever before. Our sales rose 45%!

Because of that work, I commissioned him to re-do our website to include more passive income opportunities for our company and streamline our business efficiencies such as a training portal for our clients and a membership area. The results have been tremendous and our business is operating on autopilot. Michael Gerber's E Myth System at its best!

Mark is very easy to work with. He is accessible, returns his calls and e mails, unlike some of these young tech gurus who do not possess the proper business etiquette.

I would highly recommend Mark for your marketing and business growth strategy needs."

- David Grier, MBA
Baton Rouge, Louisiana

"Recently I was introduced to Mark Mathis and his companies from a friend in the home inspection business. He told me how he increased his production by 40% the following month he used him. Who couldn't use a 40% increase in these times, he said?

After my initial conversation & presentation from Mark I knew he was the man to help my company with growth. His ideas and materials are state of the art and looking forward to working with him for years to come.

I would recommend him to any company who wants to see their numbers increase. He is about professionalism and production and that is a key to growth for any company."

- Thomas Jones
Lake Charles, Louisiana

"About six months ago, I was spending several hundred dollars per month, on average, on pay-per-click advertising. I was also having to take time to manage my Google and Microsoft/Yahoo pay-per-click accounts.

After working with Mark for a very short time, he was able to bring my search results presence to the first page, and best of all, my website was on the front page when using the most significant search term.

Local Marketing Labs has helped me to develop a sustainable marketing program that brings in new leads and prospects on auto-pilot.

I have another company that I continued to use pay-per-click. I asked Mark to do the same treatment to this other website (different search terms).

Business jumped up, and I am currently suspending my pay-per-click campaign for that business, as well, because I have more business than I can handle.

I would highly recommend Mark and his companies to ANY business owner who is looking for a "better way" to increase profits and to generate new customers on monthly basis."

- Gerard Duhon P.E.
Houston, Texas

"Mark and his entire team have been integral in getting me positioned at the top of many local search engine rankings, and have been responsible for generating clients to my business, along with customer leads. If you are interested in increasing your online presence, give Mark a call. It's guaranteed…"
- David Humphreys
Baton Rouge, Louisiana

"Today, people are so bombarded with information that advertising can be tough and seem ineffective. More and more people are going to the Internet, but if you are not the head of an IT department, you most likely have no clue how to use this tool effectively.

Foxy's Fitness Centers began working with Mark and his company a little more than a month ago, and he makes marketing on the internet easy to understand. Their video tutorials are innovative and effective in helping the average person understand how Internet marketing works.

Best of all, in just a few weeks Foxy's has seen measurable results such as being ranked much more highly on the search engines, and by being able to connect with our prospects in a much more "real" way, through the use of their videos.

Mark also actively seeks new ideas relevant to your business's needs, not just with Internet searches, but also with your website, customer retention, customer service, and data collection processes.

So if you want to begin marketing on the Internet, but have no clue how to get started or what even works, call Mark at Local Marketing Labs. He will make it simple to understand, and he will develop a plan to help you based on what your business needs."

- Josh Barnett
Baton Rouge, Louisiana

"Dear Mark,

I wanted to send you a note thanking you for your recent work done to raise our web search number. It was amazing how we went from the bottom 1000's to in the top 10 with your help.

The proposal you sent for an ongoing marketing plan is very through and comprehensive. We are currently discussing the potential and expect to make a decision shortly.

I think the ideas you have will set our company apart from our competition. The marketing plan looks great and the price I think is fair.

Thank your for your help and I look forward to a lasting business relationship. I would gladly recommend your services to a business colleague or friend."

- Kevin Dinkel
Baton Rouge, Louisiana

"Mark Mathis has been great for our business.

Very courteous, knowledgeable, and prompt to respond to any questions we have.

We have been using Mark to aid in improving our business in the Home Inspection Field for over 4 months and we have seen a marketable increase in our number of home inspections.

Their knowledge of the internet and ways to improve our business was money well spent."

- Jamie Schiro
Lake Charles, Louisiana

"Many of our clients seek valuable information from a simple Google search. As an industry leader in the Baton Rouge area, we cannot rest on our laurels when it comes to modern marketing.

Before we partnered with Mark and Local Marketing Labs, we were lost in the clutter of similar websites that may or may not had anything to do with our industry.

Thanks to Mark and the team at Local Marketing Labs for helping increase our internet presence."
- Scott Lanehart
Baton Rouge, Louisiana

"Working with Mark was fantastic. Everything was done as promised, in a timely manner, and turned out better than expected. Thanks again Mark!"

\- Sherri L. Weaver
Kansas City, Missouri

"Mark has transformed my business by effectively marketing my company's services to a more broad and diverse audience.

Their prompt and professional staff could be an asset to anyone who is fortunate enough to partner with them…"

\- Wayne Dyer
Zachary, Louisiana

"Great advice, love the free stuff, experienced eCommerce guys like yourself sharing info is great. Many thanks"

\- Gary Davis
Auckland, New Zealand

"Excellent information and very good instructions! Thank You!"

\- David De Broveck
San Jose, California

"I have learned a lot from the free e-Commerce videos. I am starting out with a web site that cost $24 a year so I don't get much from a search engine advertisement but Mr. Mathis showed me in the video how to get around that. I plan on getting more attention later but I wanted to get some clientele first. I have a few customers and growing."

- Stoney Gregg Mullins
Jacksonville, Florida

"Mark is an inspiration, great content from this guy every time."

- Gordon Lee Smith
London, England

"Mark really does a great job with his videos. Very straightforward and loaded with helpful information... Thanks!!!"

- Steve Dickinson
Massachusetts

"I have found Mark to provide in depth, informative, and easy to understand information, that is comprehensive and practical. There is such a wealth of information available, but this the material I have either read or watched from Mark has been directly useful and to the point. He is also approachable and responsive which makes for a winning combination."

- David Bay
North Carolina

"Mark is very knowledgeable in his field and I will definitely use his services."

- Frank Pitkat
Jacksonville, Florida

"Mark has been quite helpful in answering advanced eCommerce related questions."

- Dick Koroki
Gardena, California

"Mark's eCommerce trainings always provide helpful information and ideas useful for all types of businesses!"

- Lisa V.

"Mark is well informed and highly experienced. He is great at breaking down his knowledge into easy to logical steps that are understood and follow. He'll help you avoid a lot of wasted time because he has already helped invent this wheel!"

- Katharine Cotrell
Portland, Oregon

"Mark has been generous with his knowledge and time. He has also provided valuable feedback on my new online store. Needless to say he is quite a expert on eCommerce."

- Dick Koroki
Gardena, California

"I have learned a lot from Mark through another sophisticated eCommerce marketer. He is very reputable and I have learned a lot from him."

- Nick Graff
Chicago, Illinois

"Mark has taught me quite a bit from his website and I look forward to learning more."

- Terry Cole

Joplin, Missouri

"I've learned a tremendous amount from Mark. His tutorial videos are awesome to help you understand the program and he offers personal assistance when you need it most!!! Thanks Mark and for eCommerceSiteOwners.com for helping us manage our company!!!"

- Lisa Vaughan

Baytown, Texas

"Mark Mathis has been super helpful in answering my biggest concerns. His training videos are top-notch! I wouldn't want to start an eCommerce store without learning from Mark."

- Kay Donato

Florida

"Fills in the missing knowledge pieces. Often more practical oriented than other how to sessions. Keep it up, Mark"

- Anna Nosek

Vancouver, Canada

"Mark is great! Timely responses as well as in depth knowledge on this topic of online web business."
- Harold Stewart

"I liked the way Mark delivered in clear terms that I as a newer marketer could follow."
- Dave Market

"I currently have two eCommerce stores. One is a work in progress, but your funding your life with eCommerce video has inspired me to build more sites to fund my life and my future dreams."

"Very informative, eye opening and very motivating"

"Mark seems to genuinely care for his customers. I would have no doubts about getting his training."

"I have found Mark to be very knowledgeable. He produces high quality and informative content."

"Quality information, with Marks expertise I look forward to developing my skills to succeed in my new venture."

"Mark has inspired me with the courage to venture into the world of eCommerce."

LAST CHANCE!
REGISTER YOUR BOOK TO CLAIM YOUR $717.00 IN FREE BONUSES

I want to reward you for taking action and ordering this book. It shows me that you're serious and committed to growing your business, and I want to give you OVER $700 WORTH OF FREE BONUSES to help you really accelerate your growth.

Your FREE "Fast Action" Bonuses Include:

- Access to downloadable PDF version of this book, so you can print out and read anywhere! *[REAL VALUE: $29.00]*

- Access to over 2 hours of additional training in the 13 part video series where Mark walks you through the entire book, mind maps, and key takeaways. *[REAL VALUE: $297.00]*

- Access to downloadable PDF of the detailed mind map from the book - "How to Maximize the ROI of Every Single Visitor to Your Online Store" *[REAL VALUE: $97.00]*

- Access to the Previously-Unreleased video - "How to Access a VIRTUALLY UNLIMITED Database of your PERFECT Clients…" *[REAL VALUE: $97.00]*

- Free 30 Day Trial Membership & Access to our PRIVATE, "Members-Only" eCommerceSiteOwners.com "Platinum Elite" Coaching Program Website, where you can access the entire training program, including case studies, videos, tutorials, articles, marketing collateral, lead generation ideas, and MUCH more! *[REAL VALUE: $197.00]*

- **** Total REAL VALUE of Bonuses:** *$717.00* ******

To Claim your FREE Bonuses, it's simple! Just forward a copy of your order receipt email (*from Amazon or Barnes & Nobles*) to bookbonus@ecommercesiteowners.com. When we receive your receipt, we'll send you an email with the webpage to access your FREE gifts!

"May God Bless Your Family and Business"...

As we wrap up, I want you to personally know that I sincerely appreciate your business, and am always here to help.

You can do it, and I believe in you...

Thanks for checking out my book, and I hope you have blessed day,

Mark Mathis

www.ingramcontent.com/pod-product-compliance
Lightning Source LLC
Chambersburg PA
CBHW051805170526
45167CB00005B/1884